Social Unrest
in the
Late Middle Ages

medieval & renaissance texts & studies

Volume 39

Social Unrest in the Late Middle Ages

Papers of the Fifteenth Annual Conference
of the Center for Medieval and Early Renaissance Studies

Edited by

Francis X. Newman

Medieval & Renaissance Texts & Studies
Binghamton, New York
1986

Library of Congress Cataloging-in-Publication Data

State University of New York at Binghamton. Center for Medieval
and Early Renaissance Studies.
  Conference (15th : 1981)
  Social unrest in the late Middle Ages.

  (Medieval & Renaissance texts & studies ; 39)
  1. Social history — Medieval, 500–1500 — Congresses.
2. Peasant uprisings — Europe — Congresses.   3. Black death —
Congresses.   4. Europe — Moral conditions — Congresses.
I. Newman, F. X.,   II. Title.   III. Series.
HN11.S73 1981   303.6'2'094   85–28420
ISBN 0–86698–071–7 (alk. paper)

This book is set in Baskerville typeface,
with Libra display type, smythe-sewn and
printed on acid-free paper to library specifications.
It will not fade, tear, or crumble.

Printed in the United States of America

Contents

Introduction

THE ESSAYS IN THIS VOLUME were originally presented at the
Fifteenth Annual Conference of the Center for Medieval
and Early Renaissance Studies of the State University of New
York at Binghamton on October 15–17, 1981. The occasion for
the conference was the six-hundredth anniversary of the so-called
"Peasants' Revolt" that convulsed England in the summer of 1381.
The topic of the conference, however, was not the revolt itself, but
the wider context of social unrest that became so marked throughout
Europe in the latter half of the fourteenth century. It was a time
of apparently unending war, of widespread plague, of scandalous
discord in the Church—a time when the moral authority of traditional leadership was in question and even the very life of the body
itself seemed in constant and mysterious peril. Outbreaks of civil
violence like that of the English workers in 1381, or of the Jac-
querie in France, or of the *ciompi* in Florence, were only the most
dramatic manifestations of the feelings of discontent and insecuri-
ty that were stirring the peasants and artisans of Europe.

Although the essays that follow are completely independent of
each other and deal with distinctly different topics, there are threads
of common concern that link them significantly. One of the most
prominent of these motifs is the stress on the way that expressions
of social unrest were shaped by existing views of what society was
and what kinds of action were possible within it. The essays develop
a corollary point as well. In our effort to understand the turmoil
of the later Middle Ages, it is imperative for us to attend very
carefully to the way that our assumptions about society and social
action may differ from those of the people immediately involved
in the events.

Russell Peck, for example, asks us to reconsider the customary
opposition that we make between the violently subversive social
protest of a John Ball and the cooler, more detached, and essen-

tially conservative social criticism of a Geoffrey Chaucer. Peck argues that Chaucer and other literary figures who were linked to what we now call "the establishment" were echoing and in effect promoting the kind of revolutionary ideas that John Ball preached so scandalously. What gives a finally subversive force to the satire of Chaucer and others is, in Peck's view, its participation in a penitential movement that rejected politics and stressed the importance of personal conscience. While this emphasis on private and individual moral authority was apparently conservative in its eschewing of overt political concern, its ultimate effect was a subversion of the moral authority of traditional political structures. Peck contends that in the decades following the Peasants' Revolt there was, in fact, a basic change in "the medieval psyche," a new emphasis on personal conscience that foreshadows the stress on individual liberty so central to later political reform movements. Despite the obvious differences among Ball, Wycliffe, Langland, Chaucer, and Gower, they all participate, Peck contends, in this profound shift of attitude.

A very different problem of perception and interpretation is the subject of John B. Friedman's essay. Although it is clear that plague deaths in Europe after 1349 constituted a calamity of monstrous proportions, there are almost no contemporary depictions of those deaths in manuscripts or wall paintings. We are disappointed that we cannot see what the eyewitnesses to the plague themselves saw. But, as Friedman shows in careful detail, the way that artists "saw" was a function of what their existing artistic vocabulary allowed them to depict. Rather than recording the literal facts of the plague "directly," medieval artists expressed their vision of the mass affliction indirectly: either by depictions of the omnipresence of death in conventional motifs like the Dance of Death, the Three Living and the Three Dead, or the ravaged corpses of the *transi* tombs, or else by images of the supposed causes of plague or of the saintly intercessors who offered protection from it. While we may feel that there are missing images of the plague, the medieval artists themselves apparently found the existing repertoire of death images adequate to express their apprehensions.

D. W. Robertson, Jr. asks a similar question: how did the post-plague years appear to those living through them? What he shows is that for many of the most observant Englishmen of the late fourteenth century the crucial explanations for the disorder around them were not economic or political, but moral. The men whom Robertson cites — bishops, members of Parliament, poets, the king himself — saw society as bonded together by mutual concern for what was called "common profit." When these men saw society in turmoil they attributed the chaos to moral failure: to corruption and favoritism in the court, to venality in the Church, to "extortionate" wage and price demands in the third estate. Robertson's analysis of the *Canterbury Tales' General Prologue* as an image of a world in a state of moral collapse, turned almost completely upside-down by cupidity, bears comparison with Peck's stress on the new prominence of the individual conscience. Both essays emphasize a pronounced shift away from traditional social values toward what Peck calls "individualism." Though the corrupt and selfish behavior criticized by the moralists that Robertson quotes is almost the polar opposite of Long Will's anguished resort to a demanding Conscience, there is in each an emphasis on personal autonomy that undermines a value system that prized community and authority.

The two historians among the essayists, Barbara Hanawalt and J. Ambrose Raftis, both call attention to a significant problem in the interpretation of events like the uprising of 1381. As Raftis observes, peasant movements are "silent" in that those directly involved do not leave written records of their actions and attitudes. He also notes R. B. Dobson's observation that our understanding of the Peasants' Revolt is inevitably affected by the fact that the original sources of information about it are chronicles by contemporaries who were largely hostile to the rebels. Clearly, interpreting the popular social unrest of the later Middle Ages on the basis of documents that were created by the established authorities and their sympathizers is likely to lead to unbalanced conclusions. What Hanawalt and Raftis seek to do is to overcome the "silence" of the unlettered peasants and to place the revolt in the context of a freshly explored peasant culture.

Hanawalt begins with the simple problem of why, given the manifest oppression experienced by the peasantry in England and given further their overwhelming numerical superiority, they did not quickly overthrow the elite oppressing them. What she shows in the course of her paper is that peasant resistance, though persistent and effective throughout the late fourteenth century, was always expressed in ways that the peasants could conceive being implemented. People cannot engage in revolutions that they cannot imagine. So peasants resorted to law, engaged in acts of local violence, refused labor services, and thwarted their masters as best they could, but they had no vision of alternative political or economic structures. The climactic moments of the 1381 uprising revealed this very clearly when the rebels, with the capital completely in their power, put all their trust in the king, a boy-king at that, for redress of their grievances. Hanawalt sees the Peasants' Revolt as only the most dramatic manifestation of a widespread peasant resistance, but she argues that it was not a revolutionary will to change that altered peasant circumstances, but the operation of economic and social processes of which the peasants were not really aware.

Like Hanawalt, Raftis believes that the revolt of 1381 was simply "the tip of the iceberg" of worker unrest in English society. But his focus is on the way that peasant culture, accommodating itself to local circumstances, local problems, and local opportunities, was responsible for the reshaping of class relationships in society. In particular, he notes the widespread substitution of rental payments for labor services as a symptom of a new impersonality in socio-economic relations. Since these impersonal arrangements were primarily the result of peasant initiative, Raftis argues that it was the peasants, not their masters, who led the way in the development of a new pattern of class relationships in the later Middle Ages. He therefore calls for the use of the methods of social anthropology and other disciplines in an effort to uncover the reality of the social revolution that occurred among the peasantry in the century following the Black Death. Such an effort will be a corrective to the traditional tendency to assume that political or economic elites are the responsible agents of significant change, a tendency that overlooks the reality of peasant culture.

Though the occasion of the conference at which these papers were presented was an event, the focus of the conference was not so much on *what* took place as on why it took place as it did. The papers address that issue in various ways, but each demonstrates that events are shaped by the particular ways that people understand who they are and what kind of actions are open to them. Whether those understandings are traced in manuscript illustrations, or in satirical poems, or in manorial court records, or in lists of holidays, it is clear that to interpret the social unrest of the later Middle Ages intelligently we must first attend to how those involved in that unrest interpreted themselves.

FRANCIS X. NEWMAN

University Center at Binghamton

Social Unrest
in the
Late Middle Ages

Social Change versus Revolution: New Interpretations of the Peasants' Revolt of 1381

J. A. Raftis

THIS PAPER BEGINS with a brief presentation on the failure of historians to advance our understanding of the Peasants' Revolt of 1381. This failure is credited to the concentration by scholars on the concept of "revolt." In the second, and main part of this paper, some illustrations are taken from current studies of the English peasantry to suggest that now for the first time it is becoming possible to set out a peasant culture proper as the background to the Peasants' Revolt. In the third and last section of this paper some implications of the existence of the peasant culture are tested for assistance in our understanding of the Peasants' Revolt of 1381 in England.

I.

According to the excellent monograph of R. B. Dobson,[1] the main historiographical tradition on the Peasants' Revolt of 1381 has reached a stalemate: "More precisely, our knowledge of the Peasants' Revolt is irrevocably controlled and restricted by the interests and thought-sequence of its contemporary historians."[2] "Unfortunately, the evidence of indictments and pardons confronts the modern student of the revolt with problems of interpretation almost as difficult as those presented by the chroniclers."[3] "... the traditional description of the 1381 rising as a 'Peasants' Revolt' (although retained in this book because of its familiarity) is itself deceptive."[4] "Granted the difficulties of ever understanding the economic condition and social aspirations of the medieval peasant and townsman, it is hardly surprising that nearly all the most recent discussions of the great revolt have tended to stress its political causes."[5] And so forth.

Dobson's critique does not suggest that new theoretical approaches have been lacking. Marxist or neo-marxist theories of revolution have provided the main input at this level. The work of Rodney Hilton is pre-eminent in this respect.[6] Recently, social science concepts derived from more contemporary data have provided additional theoretical critiques. Although it would not seem that we are at the end of the age of ideology every theory continues to require revision. In this respect for example, George Rudé's approach[7] is a great advance over the Malthusian doctrine of traditional economic history theory that implicitly removes the physical capacity for revolt.[8] For the historian, however, there is the further frustrating problem that every theory is a period-piece, that is to say, it is derived from a particular place and time that is not mediaeval. For example, those "primitive rebels"[9] can be found in the Middle Ages, too. But "primitive" ought not to be more acceptable to mediaevalists than it is to anthropologists.[10] So, the state of the question is left unsatisfactory. To take another example, the food riot evidence so basic to the reconstruction of George Rudé could have theoretical application to earlier centuries. But how precise could this be when our economic history of a period like fourteenth-century England is shot through with obsolete negative concepts, such as the development of a money economy, or inadequately recognized realities, such as the existence of a vital regional economy?

A general answer to this problem of theory could be to remove all evolutionary elements from the theory. In the matter under consideration here, this would mean that we give the Peasants' Revolt of 1381 full status as a revolt. We could take one of the best known studies of revolution in America, for example, Crane Brinton's *Anatomy of Revolution.*[11] Brinton's threefold assessment of the symptomatic elements of a successful revolution sounds like a summary of traditional historiography of the Peasants' Revolt of 1381:

1) Structural Weaknesses, economic and political. Society is on the upgrade economically; it is the government which finds itself in financial difficulties, not the societies themselves. The prospering groups in society feel restraint, cramp, and annoyance rather than downright oppression; they feel that the government's policies limit or hinder their economic activity. The government itself is inefficient, with a chronic need for money, and efforts made to reform the machinery of government have proved unsuccessful.

2) The Transfer of Allegiance of the Intellectuals. More than
the mere alienation of the intellectuals, this element of the pre-revolutionary milieu sees the intellectuals transferring their allegiance
from the government to "another and better world" than that of
the corrupt and inefficient old regimes. The rise of a competing
"ideology" and anti-government propaganda is closely tied to this
trend.

3) Bitter Class and other Antagonisms. The ruling class is seen
to be divided and inept, unable to fulfill its function in society, and
there is more antagonism between the classes than is usual. Members of the ruling class tend to distrust themselves and some transfer their allegience to the lower classes. The rising prosperity of
the lower classes leads them to resent being shut out from the higher
social distinctions of the upper class; as the classes come closer
economically, the social barriers seem more artificial and hateful.
Increased class conflict and resentment is the result.

However, Crane Brinton, or more recently scholars such as Barrington Moore, would not include the Peasants' Revolt of 1381
within their historical purview of revolutions (English Glorious,
American, French and Russian) because they would consider this
revolution unsuccessful.[12] At this juncture, the historian in us bris-
tles again. For what is a successful event, whether a war or revolution or a less violent form of change, must surely be judged within
the context of the society of the time. Brinton, Barrington Moore
and others reject a revolt such as that of 1381 as not worthy of the
name because in the final analysis their criterion of change is the
politicized social structure. But certainly, improvements in the condition of the peasantry over the hundred years after the Black Death
have become acknowledged as a "successful event."[13]

In short, the heavy concentration upon theory to the virtual ex-
clusion of new historical research in this century has become something of a vicious circle for the Peasants' Revolt of 1381 as for other
revolts and revolutions.[14] Concepts are of course real elements of
the past, but we are just beginning to appreciate the hardening
of social concepts in late mediaeval Europe.[15] And our critical
awareness of the role of concepts in peasant historiography is still
in its infancy when we have not even assessed the historians' biases
in the study of the peasant of pre-revolutionary Russia.[16] In the
meantime, R. B. Dobson did indeed seem to acknowledge that we
might break out of the circle by treating the English peasantry in-

dependently as a historical society[17] and he recognized some be-
ginnings of such treatment when he was compiling his study in the
late 1960s. Since that time, studies of the fourteenth-century peasantry of England have increased dramatically. While much still remains to be done before a definitive picture of this peasantry can
be drawn, the existence of a genuine peasant culture is becoming
incontestable.

II.

In the context of traditional English historiography the use of
the term "peasant" to designate the Peasants' Revolt of 1381 was
a misnomer. For the traditional mediaeval economic and social
historian did not speak of peasants. Rather, he spoke of the various
classes in Anglo-Saxon society[18] and, after the full-blown establishment of the manorial system, of free and unfree. The free were
studied under such titles as sokemen by legal historians and in relation to freehold by economic historians.[19] The unfree were normally designated as villeins[20] although economic historians found
the class specification by services of virgaters, half-virgaters and
various smallholders to be more practical.

This traditional historiography is still in place. However, over
recent decades a parallel set of studies has been gradually developing. Such studies are the product of many specializations unfamil-
iar to traditional historiography. Moreover, conceiving themselves
as sharply focussed scientists, these scholars evince little interest
in the conceptual theories sketched above in Section I. Rather, they
are content to let their research findings fall into place alongside
their scientific peers in modern and early modern studies. It is not
yet possible, therefore, to assess the impact of such recent studies
on the future historiography of the English mediaeval peasant.
Nonetheless, the findings of this new research are too suggestive
for the background of the Peasants' Revolt to be overlooked. The
following paragraphs offer some preliminary probings from these
new studies.

Although it does violence to our long-cherished evolutionary sensibilities to look upon the economic base of most mediaeval English villages — the open-field system — as other than irrational, to
conceive of a village society worthy of the name as co-existing with
the manorial system, to imagine that there was a scope for decision-
making, leadership and family life, this is precisely what historians
are now able to do.

Two young American scholars, Carl Dahlman[21] and Donald McCloskey,[22] are leading the way towards establishing a rationale for the open-field system. Paradoxically, it is the sophisticated new economic theory, with a system analysis capable of including more factors than traditional theory, that has enabled scholars to isolate this relative viability of the open-field system. Piece by piece scholars are extending and detailing the rational scope of the peasants' economic activities. Bruce Campbell finds evidence for intensive farming as part of the village scene in England as on the Continent.[23] John Langdon has established that the use of horses rather than oxen by villagers is easily explicable in the versatility of horse-power for the peasant.[24] Preliminary findings by Christopher Dyer and John Langdon in a major research project on the harnessing of power by mills indicate that mills became part of peasant holdings by the thirteenth century rather than monopoly tools of exploitation by the lords.[25]

The capacity for economic decisions required a certain degree of self-government. A highly articulated local government system served the villagers as well as the lord through elected jurors and reeves together with lesser officials such as beadles, haywards and ale-tasters. Byelaws were obviously of economic significance to the whole village and so were dictated by the whole village. Most likely the lords were more concerned with the possibility of profit in the entire system than with coercive control over its several parts. Such indeed was the case even for royal manors or small towns such as Havering[26] and Godmanchester[27] as well as by the lords throughout pastoral and woodland regions along with the more developed open fields of the champion regions. A forthcoming study verifies that the abbot of Ramsey judiciously avoided taking profits from the fines at the fair of St. Ives in order to further the success of the fair.[28]

Such economic and organizational responsibilities indicate a viable society. By the late thirteenth century this society becomes visible in our records. Individual peasants appear by name in history whether one so identifies them by the common sense approach[29] or by the limited demographic data available to the medievalist.[30] From these identifications one may see that leadership qualities were recognized for the major roles of reeves and jurors in all villages. Those local power groups to be found everywhere in peasant history were obvious in mediaeval England.[31] Family structures were strengthened by ecclesiastical marriage laws,[32] and by various strategies employed in last wills and testaments, as well as by the interaction of family networks.[33]

There is nothing in these recent studies that idealizes or romanticizes either the English peasant or his community. These villagers were no more or less perfect than those of other societies. For that type of society, they were very normal in their excessive suspicion and aggression against outsiders, whether from far or near. They were capable of directing morality and law towards the support of certain elite concerns, as in the imposition of penalties against extra-marital sexual activity solely for the protection of wealthier families.[34]

In short, English villages apparently had a full-blown peasant capacity to react against conditions affecting their lives. In contrast with the law-abiding ideal of the modern citizen, this peasant behavior may seem to us not to be law-abiding or at least to be truculent in the face of public law. Scholars argue that this does not mean a disrespect for the law[35] but a different social psychology founded upon the more immediate scope of law in daily life. For example, there were so many fixed fines for failures in work services that at times these seem to have become a regularized form of commutation from the side of the peasant at least; and certainly scholars have been able to explain the small repetitive fines for brewing improperly only as licences to brew for the public.

This capacity for expressing opposition within the system or of containing violence, if you will, has too readily been taken by traditional historiography as an indicator that peasants were non-violent, submissive people. By her pioneer studies of gaol delivery rolls Barbara Hanawalt has disabused us of this false deduction.[36] Comparative data on violence in different periods of history are not very useful[37] unless one can allow for comparative institutional efficiencies in restraining and redirecting violence. Peasant capacity for absorbing violent types is dramatized by the return to their former communities of criminals convicted of homicide after these had been granted amnesty for serving in the king's army. In addition, those most prominent in peasant village government could direct violence for their own purposes.[38] This complex issue may be best illustrated by an example. On 10th June, 1332, William Colion and Andrew Bonis of Godmanchester were charged before William *le* Moigne, sheriff of Huntingdon at his tourn in Toseland, with murdering John *de* Raveley, parson of All Saints Church in Hunting-don. Along with Colion and Bonis eighteen other men were charged with aiding and abetting: Simon Parson, Richard his son, John Hardy, taylor, John Notting, smith, Gilbert son of John Notting, Robert Denne, clerk, Godfrey Manipenny, Thomas Hopay, John Godman, John Hilde, Henry son of Reginald, son of John Hilde, William son of Alan *le* Mileward, John Baronn, Roger Manipenny, John Glewe, butcher, Andrew Mundeford, John *le* Longe, smith and Lamberois LenyWere.[39] Every one of these men held a prominent public position at Godmanchester. As was normally the case before juries of their local peers, none were indicted for the charge.

From evidence at hand from the previous hundred years, therefore, one can deduce that English peasants were perfectly capable of the violence reported in the Peasants' Revolt of 1381. Furthermore, this evidence does not support the concusion that the sporadic or isolated local nature of much of the revolt indicated a revolt manqué. Rather, one would *expect* the main elements of a revolt in fourteenth-century England to be local or regional and to have occurred under many different forms. Our available evidence on the 1381 Revolt may be but the tip of the iceberg.

It is important for our understanding of peasant performance in 1381 to realize, therefore, that adjustments or reactions to changing conditions were a traditional part of peasant life as for any living society. These changes could be violent or provoke violent reactions or revolts. But, in all this, the strength of the peasant lay in the scale of his response. That is to say, he could react against changes introduced on the local scene from local causes, regional causes or national causes, but he succeeded best when the reaction could be dictated by *his* social system. Let me elaborate.

The heart of the English peasants' social system was custom, a set of reciprocal obligations touching all levels of life. Historians have never been unaware of the existence of peasant culture or customs, as may be seen in the classic work of such legal historians as F. W. Maitland and P. Vinogradoff, and the social studies of Nellie Neilson early in this century. A sociological survey of these customs was first presented by G. C. Homans in 1941.[40] More recently an economic historian, Andrew Jones, gives us a glimpse of what resources are at hand in his study of harvest customs.[41] But, as the scattered appearance of these references illustrates, the study of peasant customs in mediaeval England is still in its infancy. We are far from having responded to the challenge of George Dalton.[42] That is to say, we are far from establishing that peasant custom must be seen not only from the side of the power of lordship but also from the countervailing context of a genuine peasant culture.

Just as our sense of justice is tied closely to our system of constitutional and statutory rights, so the peasants' sense of justice and expression of rights derived from custom. The actual operation of this customary society surfaces most frequently in the records called customals and court rolls as reciprocal or contractual obligations. Among themselves, the peasants of mediaeval England frequently operated this contractual system by mutual pledging on a day to day basis and by developing byelaws for arrangements of a more seasonal nature. One of the key issues between lord and peasants concerned shifts in labor supply in relation to land. Labor was, then as so often since, a basic need for the peasant economy. The peasant farm competed with the manorial demesne for the available labor supply. As a result, peasant labor required for the complex manorial system could only be guaranteed by a contractual system. In this, the manorial economy differs in principle from, say, the plantation system in the southern USA in the nineteenth century or the collective farm in the USSR today. By contractual system, I mean a system in which villein holdings or customary land (whether or not held by villeins) were held for payment of rents for land in fixed labor services as well as money. Correspondingly, these services varied according to the size of the land unit in question and the size of the households involved.

The end product of such a contractual arrangement is illustrated in the following table from the village of Broughton, Huntingdonshire. Behind this table lay a variety of contracts between the lord of Broughton and individual peasants. In some of these contracts nearly all work services were commuted for money rents, whereas for other lands traditional services were expected. In other contracts again, land was let for fixed short periods of time while traditional arrangements left the land to a family as a veritable inheritance. By the short-term leases the lord was getting off his hands properties left vacant after the Black Death. Variations in the sale of works show how the lord had on hand a supply of labor to cover the changing requirement of years and seasons at a time of rising wages. The peasant too was buffered against this change after the

The Structure of Villein Work Payments at Broughton

	1314–15	1342–43	1378–79	1380–81	1386–87	1392–93
Annual Works Due*	4,323	3,555	2,868	3,114	3,181	2,766
		(4,281)	(4,221)	(4,362)	(4,276)	(4,386)
Annual Works† Allocated:						
Services and Censa	839	(726)	(1,353)	(1,188)	(1,095)	(1,620)
percentage	19	17	32	27	26	36
Feast Days	712	676	332	267	296	293
percentage	16	16	8	6	7	7
Illness	48	9	0	0	5	34
Work Done	1,865	2,251	2,260	1,798	2,251	2,027
percentage	43	53	54	42	53	46
Work Sold	868	636	521	1,049	630	412
percentage	20	15	12	24	15	9
Autumn Works Due	1,525	1,131	961	999	1,020	861
		(1,362)	(1,412)	(1,386)	(1,385)	(1,365)
Autumn Works Allocated:						
Services and Censa	246	(231)	(451)	(387)	(365)	(504)
percentage	16	17	32	28	26	37
Feast Days	179	104	104	22	23	39
percentage	12	8	7	2	2	3
Illness	8	4	4	0	27	8
Work Done	802	810	770	802	805	682
percentage	53	58	55	58	59	50
Work Sold	291	212	84	175	166	133
percentage	19	16	6	13	12	10

*The bracketed figures in this line include the works owed from services and *ad censum* lands, that is, the addition of the bracketed data of the next line, which data were not calculated in the summations at the end of the rolls for these years. All figures and percentages in this table have been rounded.

†Except for the year 1314–15, the total works accounted for every year tally almost exactly with the totals owed, so the totals of allocated works are not entered in this table.

See, J. A. Raftis, "Structure of Commutation on a Fourteenth-Century Village" in *Essays in Medieval History presented to Bertie Wilkinson*, eds. T. A. Sandquist and Michael R. Powicke (Toronto, 1969), pp. 282–300.

plague because the price for which he "sold" his service remained the same throughout the period of this table. The traditional contractual arrangement had, of course, buffered the peasants' lives in other ways. This point may be readily deduced from the work days allowed for religious feasts in the village of Broughton. During the winters and summers of 1314–1315 and 1342–1343 sixteen percent of the total work service owed was canceled because of religious feasts.

The fact that the peasant responded through his local social system ought not to be taken to imply that the peasant's life was bounded by the local scene. More than a generation ago Robert Redfield did much to correct our misunderstandings on this point by introducing the notion of peasant society as part of a greater society.[43] For the peasant under study here, Cicely Howell has demonstrated brilliantly that our image of the pre-industrial village as closed is the product of early modern rather than mediaeval development: "Thus it was that by the close of the seventeenth century Kibworth had been transformed into the typical 'closed' village, with a small circle of gentlemen and yeoman farmers, a growing number of craftsmen and tradesmen, a few husbandmen or small farmers and a group of landless labourers for whom housing was provided by their employers."[44]

The peasants' ability to adapt to change on the regional level is most easily demonstrated in relation to specialized trades or occupations. While some of these were local and peripheral to a village economy, many were reflective of powerful regional forces. There is plenty of evidence from the thirteenth century for the dependence of villages and small towns upon the new clerical elite as well as regional tradesmen and merchants. But there is also clear evidence that the peasant could control this situation.

Peasant responses to these regional types were on two levels. First, from the point of view of credit, the peasant was himself tied into a regional system and required legal assistance for the management of debts. Land, labor and related services were as much at the basis of wealth as was liquid capital so that debts were owed widely to labor and small tenants for the performance of multi-job services.[45] A lord's jealous concern over his local court aided the peasant in this regard, for it was greatly to the peasant's advantage to have his plea advanced at minimum cost in his own manor court and with the support of his neighbors as essoiners and pledges. The well-known vigor of the local court, by contrast with the hundred and county courts, is to be explained in great part by this kind of legal service.

Secondly, the peasants' own control system dictated local leverages upon merchants, clerks, and the like through pledging and "liberty" rights analogous to similar control over such "outsiders" by borough or lordship.[46] The frankpledge system operated on the local level to vet everyone from casual labor to the wealthy seeking full access to local land and privileges. Scribes profited from the increasing demands for their services, but scribes who were successful tended to settle in the local village or town and to become part of the local elite. Court rolls show us that it was the village reeve who was responsible for the presentation before the local court of land charters covering conveyances of local land by prominent freemen of the region.

The English peasants' ability to buffer impositions on the national level is based on their traditional role in the nation. Requirements of royal justice expressed in the assize of bread and ale and the peace keeping function of the frankpledge system are well-known. But, because of that lack of attention to peasant society already noted, little study has been made of the consequences for local life of the dependence of assize, frankpledge and even coroners upon local citizens. That the system required support by the peasants was amply demonstrated in their victory over the poll tax system introduced by Edward I. Much of the study of this story — in large part by the American scholar J. F. Willard[47] — has been clarified since the main lines of the 1381 Peasants' Revolt historiography were established. For our purposes, we may note only the conclusions of this scholarship: by 1334 the Crown had conceded the assessment and collecting of the tax to local people because of the central administration's inability to control tax evasion. That the peasant was suffering from these royal impositions is now well established by J. R. Maddicott.[48] But in the early fourteenth century the peasant could react. Again, his reaction was a typically local one for it was a common custom of thirteenth- and fourteenth-century manors to have many varying obligations commuted to fixed money payments. Indeed, the model for the fixed royal tax for a village may have been that local head tax of the lord (*capitagium*) that was so often a fixed total amount from the thirteenth century to be collected by the villagers themselves.

III.

Against this background, I would like to argue that the Peasants' Revolt of 1381 was a point of dramatization in a long-term evolution of peasant society whereby many traditional flexibilities were being lost. This evolution was as much, if not more, due to deliberate decisions by the peasantry than to changes over which they had no control. But to measure the social impact of these changes is another matter, since the usual sequence in society seems to be economic and (or) technological change, emotional reaction, and only then perception of the social realities involved. (One could suggest that our industrial society is still in the first stage with respect to the social impact of computers, for example.) In addition, one of the difficulties the historian faces in measuring such change comes from the elusive nature of ritual in social lives.[49] This is particularly so for peasant life that centers on labor and, as social analysts have long known[50], labor has held an ambivalent role as both ennobling and degrading throughout western civilization.

The changed economic conditions in the background of the Peasants' Revolt have long been familiar to economic historians but the logic of the Revolt in consequence is only beginning to be understood. To put the situation most simply, impersonal account rolls and rentals were replacing customaries and related customary court rolls (and possibly account rolls)[51] after the Black Death. Accounting is much more efficient when non-accountable factors are excluded. It was to the advantage of the peasant that the lord offered him all sorts of new rental arrangements, involving more or less commutation of work service for money rent and over longer or shorter periods of time. It was practically impossible, by the same token, that these arrangements could be combined with all the customary exchanges of earlier generations. Nor would there be the emotional attachments to older arrangements, considering the large number of old family homesteads vacated by plague and the great mix of outsider families in villages. Perhaps it is significant that, unlike earlier protest actions, no appeal to custom was recorded by the peasants in 1381.

Let us look at some details to give all this more meaning. The more impersonal nature of the peasant service is most clearly seen in the *opera* accounts. Here we find that allowances for illness — our sick leave, if you will — have almost entirely disappeared in some midland villages. Most significant was the decline in feast days or holydays (holidays), with the attendant suggestion that the religious or ritual significance of work may have altered. In at least one midland village the percentage of work owed that was allowed for feast days was about one half that allowed before the Black Death.[52]

Historians have always been puzzled by the fact that the heart of the 1381 Peasants' Revolt was in Kent and Essex where labor services had long been less demanding than in other parts of the country. The simplistic explanation of the whole villeinage system as run upon power and coercion fitted ill with the evidence for greater revolt from the least coerced. The bitter reaction against vestiges of villeinage in Kent and East Anglia does fit well, however, with the explanation given above, that is to say, customary services would have least meaning where commutation was longer established. Customary tenure would have no more meaning for peasants from these eastern regions than the service of knighthood for a mercenary soldier. Allowing for the self-interest of the landed aristocracy and their chronicler spokesmen, it is possible that the chroniclers were speaking to a real change in peasant mentality in speaking of the mercenary spirit among laborers after the Black Death.

The evolution of the English peasants' condition after the Black Death is much more clearly discernible on the regional level than on the local. As a backdrop to the need to look at this evolution from the point of view of the peasant as actor, it may be recalled that evidence for the lord's ability to dispose the villein's labor services over a region is not a powerful factor in the history of the manorial economy. For example, there is much evidence for carrying service over the twelfth and thirteenth centuries, but this had to be supplemented by money or food stipends. Often, by the fourteenth century, this carrying service had been replaced by professional carters. More basic, there is no consistent evidence for any period of the lord's ability to shift customary tenants from one manor to another.

It was peasant initiative, therefore, that prescribed the new regional patterns of labor after the Black Death. The peasant responded to the higher offers for his labor beyond his home village. Even with the apparent decline in the pledging system — a voluntary organization for the most part one must assume — the local social group would have lost much of its ability and its desire to control the entry of outsiders. Those local controls that did remain frustrated newcomers who did not have traditional affections for the village.[53] But such controls were most frustrating for regional types like clerics[54] and artisans who never had as much in the way of local attachment.[55] The role of the Jack Straw type and the Wat Tyler type in 1381 could have been predicted over the previous three decades.

It almost goes without saying that if the evolution of the peasant's condition had removed much of his control over local and regional matters, these same developments would have left him with much less control over national influences. The more clearly articulated accounting, the weakening of local loyalties and the inability of the villagers to depend upon officials (reeves, for instance) as their 'men' left the peasant exposed to demands such as the poll tax. Rent rolls told it all, so small wonder that they wanted to destroy these.[56] Officials were alien forces, so it is not surprising that these were personal enemies in the Revolt and that several were killed. This is a far cry from the beginning of the fourteenth century when a villager could be openly hounded in the village court by his fellow peasants for having disclosed some of their wealth to the royal tax assessor!

A full reinterpretation of the Revolt of 1381 is beyond the purview of this essay. The Past and Present Conference of 1 July 1981, has made available a most useful recent analysis of the events themselves.[57] There is now at hand an excellent study by Christopher Dyer[58] of the peasant society newly emerging from the late fourteenth century that, parallel to the summary in Section II above, demonstrates the potential of many new specialized disciplines.

Actors in the Peasants' Revolt other than the peasants must also have further study. For example, the moral condemnations of the late fourteenth century discussed by D. W. Robertson[59] are surely part of the same frustrated reaction against change that we have noted above for the peasant. Again let us note that such moralizing tends to take place because of the vacuum left with the failure of traditional institutions. When the nature of the change has not been understood and new institutions are not yet in place to respond to the new needs following upon these economic and social changes, moralizing becomes the order of the day. It will be necessary for future historians to place the 1381 Revolt more firmly within developments *after* 1381. For example, it may well be that the massive exodus of peasants from their home villages after 1400, along with the farming of so many demesnes in the next decade or two, was the major social and economic revolution in fourteenth- and fifteenth-century England!

Insofar as positive political and (or) military action was concerned, by definition the peasant had no national political or military means at his disposal. As has been noted at the beginning of this section, English peasants were reacting against economic, legal and social change, but there is no evidence that they had acquired a national or political mentality. Scholars now seem to be agreed that the oft-quoted language of the Revolt — such as the famous couplet: When Adam delved and Eve span / Who was then the gentle- man? — had been familiar to fourteenth-century folklore for gen- erations and did not signify some new consciousness.[60] Nor would the expectations of the king appear to be more than the normal religious sentiment of the time, reflected in various ways such as the curative effects of the royal touch and the political theology of the king's two bodies.[61] And so the actual events of the Peasants' Revolt are not expressions of peasant life at all, but rather of peas- ants joining themselves to other frustrated elements in society that had some knowledge and know-how of para-military activity. The peasant was not as such a military man, though there must have been many former soldiers throughout the countryside during the Hundred Years' War, especially in such a nerve centre as Kent. At every stage and phase of the brief campaign it was apparently non-peasants who gave the leadership, the volatile tradespeople in Kent, the disaffected clergy in Essex, the politically wise towns- men in London, town against gown in Cambridge, burgher against abbey at St. Albans and Bury St. Edmunds.

In sum, we ought not to be surprised that our historiography of the Peasants' Revolt does not allow for an anthropology of the peasant, since the application of the methods of the social anthro- pologist (or related disciplines) to the study of the traditional Euro- pean peasant is quite recent, largely since World War II insofar as the English-speaking world is concerned. In any case, these studies have come along after the main theories about the 1381 Peasants' Revolt were formulated. Nor ought we to be surprised that historians have not taken this anthropological perspective into account, since English historians never really have admitted to their

ancestors being peasants! These ancestors might have been con-
quered, been enslaved, been enserfed — but peasants, no! One of
the latest illustrations of this point is to be found in Alan Macfarlane's volume, *The Origins of English Individualism.*[62] This study per-
forms a useful role insofar as it underlines the significant reality
of the individual (why individual*ism* is not clear!) in village life of
late mediaeval and early modern England. But why, by implication, these people were thereby not peasants is difficult to understand. Even with an elementary folklore knowledge of the modern
French peasant, for example, one knows how toughly individual-
istic these people still are (keeping money in the old sock!). If Alexander Solzhenitsyn's characterization of Ivan Denisovitch[63] is true,
peasant personality types are not readily changed by even modern
revolutions. But this resiliency of the peasants' social psychologi-
cal features must be distinguished from the reality of change in social and economic conditions.

What is at issue, then, is not so much the continuity of peasant
life as the degree of change that life was undergoing. This has become an issue for historians, I would submit, because peasant revolutions are "silent" revolutions.[64] Silent revolutions are not the
stuff that historians make their careers from, so this topic has been
low on our list of priorities. But the reality of this revolution is
nonetheless obvious. I would think that the greatest social revolution in the history of peasant England was the disappearance of
slavery from the end of the eleventh century. But how could this
phenomenon compete with the literary history of the Magna Carta?
In parallel fashion, I would expect that one of the greatest revolutions in the social and economic life of the English peasantry occurred during the century after the Black Death. That people of
other ways of life more likely to leave literary records were also
in a state of revolution distracts us from this peasant reality. And
so, there were indeed national forces at work in late fourteenth-
century England, such as the Hundred Years War; and there were
class political pressures, such as the Statute of Laborers. But what
were these to the ordinary lives of people? By the late fourteenth
century nearly every facet of peasant life had changed from a generation or two earlier: the bacteria attack on every family, perhaps
the weakening of the marriage bond,[65] the relative size of his tene-
ment, the nature and variety of his rents, the size and function of
the lord's property (demesne), the familiarity of his neighbors, the

local institutions in which he was involved, his relation with the parish (church wardens, guilds, possible lollardy), his relations with outsiders.

None of the traditional institutions could buffer these changes. The Peasants' Revolt was a mere ripple on the troubled surface of peasant life in late fourteenth-century England.

Notes

1. R. B. Dobson, ed., *The Peasants' Revolt of 1381*, (London, 1970) The documents are prefaced by a thirty-one page introduction.

2. Ibid., p. 3.

3. Ibid., p. 8.

4. Ibid., p. 13.

5. Ibid., p. 20.

6. See, especially, R. H. Hilton and H. Fagan, *The English Rising of 1381* (London, 1950); and Rodney Hilton, *Bondmen Made Free, Medieval Peasant Movements and the English Rising of 1381* (New York, 1973).

7. George Rudé, *The Crowd in History, a study of popular disturbances in France and England, 1730–1848* (New York, 1964).

8. For this reason, perhaps, the 1381 Revolt is played down by Postan in contrast to his emphasis on peasant conditions in the pre-Black Death period. See M. M. Postan, *The Medieval Economy and Society* (London, 1972), chap. 3.

9. E. J. Hobsbawm, *Primitive Rebels, Studies in Archaic Forms of Social Movement in the 19th and 20th Centuries* (Manchester, 1959).

10. Complaint about the use of the word primitive is a commonplace among social anthropologists. See, for example, Raymond Firth, *Elements of Social Organization* (London, 1963), p. 63 for a sensitive appreciation of early art as non-primitive.

11. Crane Brinton, *The Anatomy of Revolution*, rev. ed. (New York, 1965).

12. Barrington Moore, Jr., *Social Origins of Dictatorship and Democracy: Lord and Peasant in the Making of the Modern World* (Boston, 1966), p. 453: "The process of modernization begins with peasant revolutions that fail. It culminates during the twentieth century with peasant revolutions that succeed. No longer is it possible to take seriously the view that the peasant is an 'object of history', a form of social life over which historical changes pass but which contributes nothing to the impetus of these changes...." I would argue that Barrington Moore, Jr. confuses modernization with politicizing.

13. See, below, especially Section III.

14. Dobson, *Peasants' Revolt*, p. 11.

15. See Richard Hoffman, "Outsiders by Birth and Blood: Racist Ideologies and Realities Around the Periphery of Medieval European Culture," *Studies in Medieval and Renaissance History* 10 (1984): 3–34.

16. Esther Kingston-Mann, "Marxism and Russian Rural Development: Problems of Evidence, Experience, and Culture," *The American Historical Review* 86, no. 4 (October, 1981): 731–52.

17. Dobson, *Peasants' Revolt*, p. 1.

18. See H. P. R. Finberg, "Anglo-Saxon England to 1042" in *The Agrarian History of England and Wales*, vol. 1:2 (Cambridge, 1972), pp. 383–525.

19. For a recent example, see Edmund King, *Peterborough Abbey, 1086–1310* (Cambridge, 1973), chapter three.

20. For the most up-to-date study, see Paul R. Hyams, *King, Lords and Peasants in Medieval England: The Common Law of Villeinage in the Twelfth and Thirteenth Centuries* (Oxford, 1980).

21. Carl Dahlman, *The Open Field System and Beyond: A Property Rights Analysis of an Economic Institution* (New York, 1980).

22. See D. N. McCloskey, "English open fields as behaviour towards risk," *Research in Economic History: An Annual Compilation of Research* 1 (1976): 124–70.

23. See Bruce Campbell, "Agricultural Progress in Medieval England: Some Evidence from Eastern Norfolk," *The Economic History Review*, 2d ser., 36 no. 1 (1983): 26–46.

24. John Langdon, "The Economics of Horses and Oxen in Medieval England," *The Agricultural History Review* 30, part 1 (1982): 31–40.

25. See Christopher Dyer and John Langdon, "English Medieval Mills," *Bulletin of The University of Birmingham* (23 January 1984): 1–2.

26. See Marjorie K. McIntosh, "The Privileged Villeins of the English Ancient Demesne," *Viator* 7 (1976): 295–328.

27. See J. A. Raftis, *A Small Town in Late Mediaeval England: Godmanchester 1278–1400* (Toronto, 1982). Thirty-five different individuals were involved in the local administration of the town. The practicality of local custom extended to much later periods. See George Lee Haskins, *Law and Authority in Early Massachusetts, a Study in Tradition and Design* (New York, 1960), pp. 167ff.

28. See Ellen Wedemeyer Moore, *The Fairs of Medieval England: An Introductory Study* (Toronto, 1985).

29. Cicely Howell, *Land, Family and Inheritance in Transition: Kibworth Harcourt, 1280–1700* (Cambridge, 1983): 26–46.

30. Judith M. Bennett, "Spouses, Siblings and Surnames: Reconstructing Families from Medieval Village Court Rolls," *The Journal of British Studies,* 23, no. 1 (1983): 26–46.

31. Edward Britton, *The Community of the Vill* (Toronto, 1977), chapter one.

32. See note 65 below.

33. See Judith M. Bennett, "Gender, Family and Continuity: A Comparative Study of the English Peasantry, 1287–1349" (Ph. D. diss., University of Toronto, 1981). Richard M. Smith, "English Peasant Life-Cycles and Socio-Economic Networks: A Quantitative Geographical Case Study" (Ph.D. diss. Cambridge University, 1974).

34. See note 31 above.

35. For the most detailed study to date of the balance sought between social control and distrust in the English village, see M. Patricia Hogan, "Medieval Villainy: A Study in the Meaning and Control of Crime in an English Vil-

lage," *Studies in Medieval and Renaissance History* 2, o.s., vol. 12 (1979): 123–24.

36. Barbara Hanawalt, *Crime and Conflict in English Community, 1300–1348* (Cambridge, Mass., 1979).

37. Some salutary words of caution about the use of comparative crime data are given by Carl I. Hammer, Jr., "Patterns of Homicide in a Medieval University Town: Fourteenth-Century Oxford," *Past and Present* 78 (February, 1978): 3–23.

38. See Barbara Hanawalt, "Community Conflict and Social Control: Crime and Justice in the Ramsey Abbey Villages," *Mediaeval Studies* 39 (1977): 402–23.

39. I am indebted to Barbara Hanawalt for this information from gaol delivery rolls.

40. G. C. Homans, *English Villagers of the Thirteenth Century* (Cambridge, Mass., 1941).

41. See Andrew Jones' articles "Harvest Customs and Labourers' Perquisites in Southern England, 1150–1350: the corn harvest," *Agricultural History Review* 25:1 (1977): 14–22 and "Harvest Customs and Labourers' Perquisites in Southern England, 1150–1350: the hay harvest" 25:2 (1977): 98–107.

42. See, for example, George Dalton, "Peasantries in Anthropology and History," *Current Anthropology* 13 (1972): 385–415.

43. Robert Redfield, *Peasant Society and Culture* (Chicago, 1960).

44. Howell, *Kibworth Harcourt*, p. 69.

45. See Elaine G. Clark, "Medieval Debt Litigation: Essex and Norfolk, 1270–1490" (Ph.D. diss., University of Michigan, 1977), for the matter of this paragraph. Some of this thesis is now available in the chapter "Debt Litigation in a Late Medieval English Vill," in *Pathways to Medieval Peasants*, ed. J. A. Raftis (Toronto, 1981), 247–83.

46. See Raftis, *A Small Town in Late Mediaeval England*, pp. 76ff.

47. J. F. Willard, *Parliamentary Taxes on Personal Property* (Cambridge, Mass., 1934).

48. J. R. Maddicott, *The English Peasantry and the Demands of the Crown 1294–1341*, Past and Present Supplement 1 (Oxford, 1975).

49. See Brian Stock, *The Implications of Literacy, Written Language and Models of Interpretation in the 11th and 12th Centuries* (Princeton, 1983), chapter two.

50. Very little professional study has been done on this theme. See Sebastian de Grazia, *Of Time, Work and Leisure* (N.Y., 1962). Yet Sigmund Freud long ago called attention to this question: "Laying stress upon the importance of work has a greater effect than any other technique of living in the direction of binding the individual more closely to reality; in his work, he is at least attached to a part of reality, the human community. Work is no less valuable for the opportunity it and the human relations connected with it provide for a very considerable discharge of libidinal component impulses, narcissistic, aggressive and even erotic, than because it is indispensable for subsistence and justifies existence in society. The daily work of earning a livelihood affords particular satisfaction when it has been selected by free choice, i.e. when through sublimation it enables use to be made of existing inclinations, of instinctual impulses that have retained their strength, or are more intense than usual for constitutional reasons. And yet as a path to happiness work is not

valued very highly by men. They do not run after it as they do after other opportunities of gratification. The great majority work only when forced by necessity, and this natural human aversion to work gives rise to the most difficult social problems." *Civilization and Its Discontents*, trans. Joan Riviere (London, 1963), p. 17, n. 1.

51. Scholars are discovering significant changes in village personnel, especially the bailiffs replacing the reeve. Comparably, see the changed role of the schultz in central Europe.

52. See J. A. Raftis, *Warboys* (Toronto, 1974), pp. 197–98.

53. See J. A. Raftis, "Changes in an English Village after the Black Death," *Mediaeval Studies* 29 (1967): 158–77.

54. See Malcolm Burson, "The Early Fifteenth-Century Clergy in the Archdeaconry of Exeter: Social Origins and Roles" (Ph.D. diss., University of Toronto, 1979).

55. See Howell, *Kibworth Harcourt*, especially chapter eight.

56. No doubt the process can be illuminated as much from the centuries after 1381 as the decades before that date. See reference to enclosure books in J. N. Neeson, "The Opposition to Parliamentary Enclosures in Northamptonshire," Canadian Historical Association Conference, June 1981.

57. Past and Present Society Conference, London, July 1981.

58. Christopher Dyer, *Lords and Peasants in a Changing Society: The Estates of the Bishopric of Worcester, 680–1540 (Cambridge, 1980), chapter 5ff.*

59. See *infra*, pp. 49ff.

60. The Robin Hood myth is but one example of this mentality.

61. See E. H. Kantorowicz, *The King's Two Bodies: A Study in Mediaeval Political Theology* (Princeton, 1957).

62. Alan Macfarlane, *The Origins of English Individualism* (New York, 1978).

63. Alexander Solzhenitsyn, *One Day in the Life of Ivan Denisovitch* (New York, 1963).

64. Apparently, much of the history of local opposition to the enclosure movement has been missed by historians for this reason. See Neeson, "Opposition to Parliamentary Enclosures."

65. See M. M. Sheehan, "The Formation and Stability of Marriage in Fourteenth-Century England: Evidence of an Ely Register," *Mediaeval Studies* 33 (1971): 228–63.

Peasant Resistance to Royal and Seigniorial Impositions

Barbara A. Hanawalt

THE ESTABLISHED ORDER OF SOCIETY, economy and politics of medieval Europe was that of a small elite controlling the land and the people on it. It was an order of life that predated the Middle Ages, that came into existence as soon as the majority of men in the society turned their hands from hunting and fighting to plowing. With the introduction of the plow, men replaced women in grain production and those men who continued to fight and rule came to dominate the plowmen.[1] If there was a humiliation in taking over women's work that led to peasant men's passivity, we will never know. But by the fourteenth century both peasant and elite accepted the arrangement as the natural order and both regarded departures from it as major disturbances. The system was, of course, oppressive and one may wonder why the peasants, who far outnumbered the lords, did not rise up more frequently. Clearly the force of tradition and the lack of alternative models of economic and political organization were far more forceful in restraining the peasants than the armor, fighting skills, and castles of the ruling class. Even when the peasantry made significant conquests in 1381, they were easily cowed by their own fears of brutal revenge and surrendered readily. In spite of the peasants' essentially conservative views, however, they did offer resistance to the demands of lords and kings. This paper will investigate the methods they used to try to win some freedoms within the established traditions or to rid themselves of extraordinary oppressions both before and during the Great Revolt.

Rebellions against established authorities provide excitement in historical writing so that it is not surprising that peasant revolt has received considerable attention. The three classic studies of the Peasant Revolt of 1381 — Edgar Powell, *The Rising in East Anglia in 1381*;

A. Réville, *Le soulèvement des travailleurs d'Angleterre en 1381*; and Charles Oman, *The Great Revolt of 1381* — all described the events of the Revolt and placed blame for it on the poll tax and on the enforcement of the Statute of Laborers.[2] None of these authors was sympathetic with the peasants for rebelling and Oman openly cheers the King and the return to law and order. Rodney Hilton has provided a counterweight to the earlier interpretations in a recent book, *Bond Men Made Free*, and an earlier article.[3] Hilton, being a Marxist historian, is openly sympathetic to the peasants and glorifies their attacks on their oppressors. Hilton has also contributed a valuable analysis of revolts against manorial authority prior to the Great Revolt and thus shows that the causes of unrest went beyond the taxations and control over laborers; they were inevitable given the extreme social, economic, and political distinctions between the oppressed peasants and the nobility. Historical research into the conditions of the peasantry in the fourteenth and fifteenth centuries now permits us to move beyond choosing sides in the struggle. It is now apparent that the peasants and their overlords had ongoing adjustments in their power relationships and not all of these were violent. Furthermore, the royal pursuit of war in Scotland and France had far more traumatic effects on the countryside than previously assumed. And, finally, one may argue that the economic dislocations brought on by the population decrease following the Black Death and other epidemics caused the real revolution in the condition of the peasantry and the abandonment of serfdom in the fifteenth century.

It is fitting to remind ourselves at the outset of the ordinary demands that lords and kings imposed on the peasantry. The legal claims on a manor by one Staffordshire lord may serve as an illustration. In 1364 Sir Thomas de Ardene laid claim in Chester court to a manor over which he swore that he had full rights. Although some of the claims were archaic, they indicate the extent of the inexorable and often capricious power of the manorial lords. For his soke he claimed for himself and his heirs the right to hold the manorial court and try all pleas of trespass, covenants, debts and detinue up to forty shillings that arose among his tenants. Not only were the villeins subject to this limitation of court, but also all freemen on the manor had to bring cases to his court as part of his soke. For his rights in toll Sir Thomas argued that he could impose arbitrary taxes on his villeins. The progeny of these villeins were not free, for even those as yet unborn belonged to him and his heirs. Among the felony jurisdictions he claimed were the out-moded infangthef, duel, and ordeal of fire and water as well as view of frankpledge and the right to maintain three sergeants of the peace at the expense of his tenants. Each tenant was to provide these officials for six weeks "with the same food as the paterfamilias resident on the land would have, or the equivalent in money."[4] Thus to add insult to injury, the peasants had to maintain the very officials who were to enforce the lord's manorial rules.

Sir Thomas was making his case for rights that the earl should grant to him in the manor; his suit did not mention the ordinary proceeds from owning the manor and the people on it. These included the annual rents that the peasantry paid for their messuage and lands; the dues in kind such as the chicken at Christmas and eggs at Easter; the regular labor services at plowing, planting, harvest and other times; the charge for getting wood from his forest; and the numerous and onerous fines and charges for every passage in a peasant's life. Merchet had to be paid for a woman's marriage, leyrwith for sexual relations before marriage, fines for entering into property rentals, fines for breaking any part of the obligations to the lord, and, finally the heriot payable with the best animal on death. For most of England, the mandatory use of the manorial court, the rents, labor services, and various fines and tallages dominated peasant life.

The system remained intact for centuries through long custom reinforced by continual meetings of the manorial courts. At the courts the lord's officers heard charges of infractions of manorial rules and the offenders were punished with fines or perhaps stocks. The usual offenses were failure to appear for work on the lord's land, failure to pay one of the fines such as merchet or land transfer fees, refusal to have grain ground in the lord's mill or to pay tallage, and trespass on the lord's property. The mere enforcement of manorial rules had two galling aspects. First, the lord made considerable profits from the court — £10 per session was not unusual. Second, other peasants were asked to report the lapses of their fellow villagers and to stand in judgment over them.

Any rules, as long as they were written down or well established by custom could be lived with more readily than arbitrary impositions. As Hilton has pointed out, it was the addition of an unaccustomed tallage or the arbitrary increase in work requirements that usually led villages to organize in revolt.[5] Furthermore, lords often employed a heavy hand in enforcing their rights over tenants. Sir Ralph Porthos of Polebrook ordered two of his henchmen to go to the house of John Weldon of Polebrook on the evening of 13 May 1301. When they arrived, they found John asleep and immediately set on him with a sword that wounded him in the head to the brain and an axe that cut into his back. They took from him ten shillings, one farthing and fled to Sir Ralph's court. The tithing men followed the hue and cry but Sir Ralph took in his two servants and excluded the tithing men. Afterwards, he spirited away his helpers. The township claimed that the reason for the attack was that John was Sir Ralph's villein and that his wife had committed an offense for which she was to be put into stocks.[6]

Seigniorial violence toward the peasantry often exhibited an arrogance of class superiority. For instance, Hugh Fitz Henry, a local lord, was charged with the rape of Maude, daughter of Ingreda Scot of Ingleton. The jurors said that Hugh was passing through the village of Ingleton one day when he saw Maude standing in her mother's doorway. He ordered two of his servants to seize Maude and take her to his manor house in the village. She fought her abductors by clinging to the doorway and raising the hue and cry, but she was eventually dragged off. The jurors maintained that once in the manor house she submitted voluntarily to him. They surely knew otherwise but were afraid to sentence the lord to be hanged. Instead they suggested that the king fine him £100, a very large sum.[7]

Calculated abuse of privilege also entered into the lords' treatment of their peasantry.

> On 3 Dec. [1274] John of Rushall, knight and his esquire Henry of Hastings were entertained at the Parson of Melchbourne's house and Henry took provisions necessary for his Lord's use from many men in Melchbourne. Those whom they owed money for food and oats came and asked to it. John and Henry said that they had no ready money in Melchbourne and asked them to send a man with them to Cambridge and [said] that they should have the ready money there. They unanimously sent Ellis of Astwood with them. Ellis followed them from Melchbourne to "le Rode" where John and Henry and others unknown of John's household cut his throat.

Sir John was eventually acquitted for his part in the theft and murder.[8]

The peasants' problems came not only from their lords, but also from the royal government. While Hilton has made much of the intrusions of the royal justices, these officials and courts were generally less oppressive than the tax collectors, recruiters, and those in charge of purveyances. After the demise of the general eyre, peasants found that they could use the criminal courts for their own ends.[9] But in the fourteenth century the crown began to rely increasingly on the population at large to support military campaigns and extra expenses. There have been three excellent studies in recent years that have dealt with the expenses incurred for warfare and the ways in which the populace suffered in paying the bill. H. W. Hewitt in *The Organization of War under Edward III* (Manchester, 1966) has written about the financing and recruiting for the Hundred Years' War while Michael Prestwick in *War, Politics and Finance under Edward I* (Oxford, 1972) has explored earlier wars. The book that deals primarily with the burdens on the peasantry, however, is J. R. Maddicott's slim volume, *The English Peasantry and the Demands of the Crown.*[10]

While taxes had been collected sporadically during the thirteenth century, in the 1290s Edward I was forced to introduce more systematic taxation to pay for his wars with Wales, Scotland, and France. After the reign of Edward I the crown assumed that the proceeds of taxation were a regular supplement to royal income. The taxes of the 1290s and the first half of the fourteenth century were based on assessments of the population's moveable property. Those with less than ten shillings worth of chattels were exempt. While the rate of assessment varied, the amount was usually a tenth to a fifteenth. Assessment was done at the local level and there was substantial underestimating and cheating that helped to lighten the burden of taxation. Nonetheless, Maddicott argues that the taxation was too heavy for some of the population to bear and that contemporary literature such as the *Song of the Husbandman* and the *Poem on the Times of Edward II* complained that taxes were taking the seed corn and that no differentiation was being made for families with many mouths to feed as compared to those with few.[11] Even if an individual round of taxation might not have been crushing, the fact that taxes were levied so frequently in the first part of the fourteenth century made them a constant drain on peasant prosperity.

When the nineth of 1341 was imposed, many contemporary observers feared that there would be a peasant revolt.[12]

As the war with France dragged on, the crown imposed taxes with increased frequency. Between 1371 and 1380 there was only one year without a general taxation. Furthermore, in order to meet the high amounts required, Parliament had to search for new ways of taxing.[13] By 1377 the king and Commons agreed to a new form of taxation that touched everyone in the land. The poll tax required a single groat from everyone. The obvious inequity of this ungraduated tax in addition to the low revenue it produced brought about a modification in 1379 in which the common laborer paid only a groat while the wealthier would pay according to a graduated scale. The tax of 1379 also did not raise sufficient revenue and so when the king asked for a substantial sum in 1380, Commons resorted to a new version of the poll tax in which as much as one shilling could be levied on even the poor members of society, only beggars and those under fifteen being exempted. As in the past there was widespread cheating and concealment of family members. The collectors produced so little that the crown had to send them back to the countryside to tax the missing people.[14] This was the straw that broke the peasants' backs and brought about the assaults on the royal tax assessors that led to the rising of 1381.

It was not simply the burden of taxation that infuriated the population, but the way in which it was being spent. The war in France turned into a series of disastrous defeats in the 1370s. While the royal armies were losing overseas, the French were sending parties of marauders to the southeastern coast of England. The Cinque Ports were besieged and raiding parties came ashore killing the local population. The king required the peasants to form a militia but neither he nor the great men of the countryside, the earl of Arundel and John of Gaunt, came to their aid. Anger against the taxation was heightened when it became generally known that funds collected in the poll tax of 1380–1381 were to go toward financing a private war of John of Gaunt's in Spain. Edmund Fryde has argued that it was taxpayer resentment over this misuse of royal funds that led to the attacks on Gaunt's property in the Great Revolt.[15]

Taxes were frequent, but they were not arbitrary. The purveyances were. When the king's household moved about its routine business through the country, the household officials collected from the native population those goods they needed to feed the entourage of people and animals. But with the wars during the fourteenth century, purveyances were used to equip armies with food, weapons, carts, and horses. Because these prises were payable in kind, the burden of providing them fell upon those counties that were closest to the military action. Thus Kent, East Anglia, and the southern coastal areas were heavily exploited to supply the army in France while Lincolnshire, Yorkshire, Huntingdonshire, and other northern counties had to provide for the periodic war with Scotland.[16] The crown was to pay for the goods so collected through the sheriffs, but the goods were given in exchange for wooden tallies that were often worthless. Numerous petitions speak of people making repeated attempts to collect their money and one poor man presented his talley to the sheriff only to have it broken in two by way of payment. Even when compensation was made, the goods were always undervalued so that full repayment was never forthcoming. Again the protest literature such as the *De Speculo Regis* of ca. 1331 claimed that the demands of the king were ruining peasants.[17]

Purveyances were not regulated through Commons so that the king's officials might go repeatedly to the same area and demand prise. Petitions to the king complained that seed corn had been taken and land was lying in waste or that half of the village plow teams had been seized and crops were six weeks late in being planted. Maddicott has estimated that if the peasant fields yielded about one quarter (eight bushels) of grain per acre, that the purveyance in Kent in 1297 alone would have taken the grain from almost 4,900 acres.[18]

The king did not stop with demanding the money and goods of the peasantry, but also required their bodies through recruitment for his armies. In areas close to battles the king had to rely upon recruits among villagers to flesh out his armies. For warfare with the Scots, therefore, Lincolnshire, Yorkshire, Cumberland, Staffordshire and other northern counties provided soldiers. Along the coastal regions as well men of the villages were called out to defend harbors against incursions of French raiders. In addition to sparing a few of their men, the villagers had to equip them with armor and weapons.[19]

It is difficult to measure the extent of damage to the peasantry that any of these royal levies produced. Certainly the areas adjacent to the fighting bore a disproportionate share of the burden. The royal demands could also cut deeply if they coincided with the periods of most intense agricultural activity — plowing and harvest. The aspects of purveyance and recruiting that made them particularly onerous were their arbitrary nature and the fact that the officials demanding these extra payments were corrupt. To these complaints were added charges that the government used the money ineptly.

A final imposition perpetrated by the royal government with the later compliance of Commons was the Ordinance of Laborers followed by the Statute of Laborers in 1351. The Black Death of 1348–1349 had left the population of England reduced by at least a third and possibly a half. Those peasants and laborers who survived the plague found themselves in a better economic position than heretofore. They could charge a reasonable market value for their labor and expect to get employment at the higher wages. Because of population reduction, men who relied on hired labor to do their planting and harvesting had no choice but to pay the wages asked. There were no other workers with whom to bargain. The speed with which the peasant laborers grasped the changed economic circumstances can be demonstrated by observing the alacrity with which the council responded to this early example of the law of supply and demand. Already by 18 June 1349 the royal ordinance was issued attempting to roll back wages to levels paid in 1346. When the first parliament met after the plague in 1351, the ordinance became a statute.

During the next thirty years, the statute was repeatedly reissued in an attempt to control prices and wages. Various judicial experiments were made trying to enforce the unpopular measure.[20] Control of wages was doomed to failure, of course, but the attempts to deprive the peasantry of this new-found prosperity raised resentments. Those who were caught and punished were obvious foes of the Statute, but so too were those who feared that they might be brought before the justices. The intention of the royal government and the Commons seemed to be that, while they reserved the right to impose frequent taxation, they were not in favor of allowing the laborers to earn a wage that would permit them to pay taxes.

Disadvantaged by long-standing subservience and the obvious superiority of the ruling elite in dealing with localized protest, the peasantry nevertheless sought various means of fighting oppression. The traditional way to escape seigniorial impositions was to

seek freedom from villein status. Villeins who had both money and
a receptive lord bought their way to freedom. The price of such
manumission was either a flat sum or more frequently the conver-
sion of services to a money rent.[21] It was also possible to simply
run away from a manor, but if the villein leased land he would
then be relinquishing this valuable source of livelihood. Usually,
the trade-off was not worth the sacrifice.

Peasants also tried to clarify their status by taking cases to royal
courts. In order to prove their freedom, the peasants had to show
that the relatives on their fathers' side had been free. Thus when
a lord in Norfolk claimed that Osbert of Waddington was his villein, he produced a number of Osbert's unfree relatives. Osbert
agreed that these relatives were unfree but that they were on his
mother's side. He produced two free first cousins on his father's
side and won the case. Not all of the peasants were so fortunate
in their claims for freedom. Ralf Potter went through an elaborate
appeal against his lord denying the legitimacy of an unfree cousin
that the lord had produced and reaching back to the free status
of his great grandfather. As he did not appear in court, he lost the
case by default.[22]

Villeins put up an equally hard legal battle in order to prove
that they belonged to another lord. The usual reason for such a
maneuver was to place themselves in the lordship of a more leni-
ent administrator.

The machinations of one family were so ingenious that the abbot of Meaux wrote down their case thirty years after it was over.
In 1356 there had been disruption in the monastery over the selec-
tion of a new abbot. The tenants had taken advantage of the temporary lapse of leadership and had revolted. Richard Cellarer was
one of the ringleaders but managed to avoid punishment by going
to the royal escheator for Holderness and claiming that he and his
family were really villeins of the king. They had wrongly gone over
to the abbot sometime before and taken their land with them. The
escheator called an inquest of villeins, who maintained that Richard was right. With his neighbors' collusion, he and his lands were
transferred to the royal demesne of Holderness. The monks protested in 1357 and by 1358 another inquisition was granted. The
jurors this time were property holders and Richard lost the case.

In 1359 John Cellarer and his cousin Thomas along with two
other members of this ambitious family made a very clever move

against the abbot. They brought a plea alleging that the abbot had violated the Statute of Laborers by taking away by force and detaining a plowman that the Cellarers had hired. The Cellarers claimed £5 each in damages. At the time of the plea the abbot was in London negotiating with the royal auditors about Richard's case. Since charges had been brought against him for violation of the Statute of Laborers, the auditors kept the abbot's horses. He was forced to rent horses in order to return home.

At the sessions of the justices of laborers the Cellarers were examined separately and admitted that they were villeins of the abbot. Being villeins, they could not bring suit against him in court. Undaunted, Richard appealed to the king for a judgment. Edward III himself ordered the sheriff to have the Cellarers and their property returned to the royal manor. The abbot made a hasty trip to London with two shrewd lawyers and some attractive gifts for the king. He was allowed to retain the Cellarers and property until the king returned from France and could make fresh inquiries.

Meanwhile, John Cellarer was imprisoned for an offense against the abbot. He managed to escape at night by crawling through a shaft in the latrine system. Once free he and a cousin tried to have their freedom from serfdom declared in court but failed.

When the king returned from France a new series of commissions investigated the case and returned the Cellarers to the abbot with their villein status intact. The decision, however, was accompanied by special instructions to the abbot that they should not be punished in any way for what they had done.[23]

As these cases indicate, the peasants showed an impressive degree of legal acumen. To bring a case into royal courts required a legal writ in Latin and a person to argue the case. Either the Cellarers had acquired this legal sophistication or they were able to hire lawyers to put together their cases for them. In either case it is apparent that they were not from the downtrodden ranks of peasantry. The family had sufficient lands that the abbot and king were willing to fight over who owned them. They were from the upper economic and social status group of the village, a group that consistently provided the leadership for revolt.

Collective cases against uncustomary increases in labor services or new tallages were also brought before royal justices for judgment. Tenants who brought a case against their lord had to make a plausible argument for a precedent that would not permit the

lord to increase his exactions. The most common basis for such
cases was to claim that the manor was part of the ancient royal
demesne. Villein tenants who lived on manors that had been demesne at the time of Edward the Confessor could claim royal protection against increased services even though the manor had sub-
sequently been alienated. The way of proving that the manor had
been part of the ancient royal demesne was a search of the Domesday Book for evidence.

A good example of an appeal to the Domesday Book comes from
the manor of Halesowen. George Homans in *English Villagers of the
Thirteenth Century* traced the legal wrangles of the tenants with their
lord, the abbot of the White Canons. In 1243 the tenants appeared
before the King's Bench at Westminister claiming that they were
free. They lost their case when they were forced to admit that they
paid merchet for the marriage of their daughters along with a number of other traditional services that proved their villeinage. Although the peasants were restive, the matter might have stopped
there if the greedy abbot had not given them another pretext for
a legal case. In 1252 the king was tallaging his royal demesne in
the region of Halesowen and the abbot, who also wanted to collect
the tallage, claimed that his manor was formerly royal demesne
and procured a writ permitting him to levy the tax. The tenants
immediately protested that the increased services that the abbot
had imposed on them were obviously illegal because, by his own
admission, the manor was part of the ancient demesne. By 1278
the tenants were withholding services in accordance with their understanding of the law. The abbot petitioned the king and his council to force his peasants to undertake the new work load, but the
king replied that the abbot should settle the matter in court in a
routine fashion. The tenants for their part had procured a writ for
the trial, but when they did not prosecute the abbot went *sine die*.[24]
In other cases the Domesday Book was actually searched to establish the legal position of the manor.[25]

Presentment of a legal case did not necessarily lead to confrontation in royal courts. On occasion peasant protest could be ac-
commodated. The most famous of these was a petition by the tenants of Bocking manor to their lord. The salutation indicates the
low-keyed nature of their protest: "To their very dear, honorable
and rightful lord, the poor tenants of Bocking pray to your lordship for grace and remedy...." The form of their petition was to

outline the duties that they had customarily rendered in court, in
the fields, in meadow, and so on and then to point out how the
new bailiff, John le Doo, had violated these customs to the detriment of the tenants. In response to this respectful remonstrance,
the prior of Christ Church, Canterbury, answered that these deeds
had been done without his knowledge and they would not happen
again in the future as long as the tenants "should maintain their
customs in all matters."[26] At no time did the tenants claim that
they did not have to render customary services. The priors treated
those who claimed to be free tenants very much the way other landlords did. They roundly denied the free status and put the ringleaders in prison.

Tenants might also be able to negotiate with their lords for ease-
ment in the manorial rules. In 1339 the tenants of Chertsey Abbey (East Surrey) under the leadership of two of their prominent
villagers, Gilbert Luwyne and Thomas Atte Hacche, went as a
group to ask the lord to change the manorial inheritance customs.
In the past the custom had been Borough English, i.e., the young-
est son inherited, but the villeins claimed that it was "to the grave
damage and detriment of the whole homage and tenants." They
requested a change to primogeniture and the abbot granted it.
Within the year three other villages followed their lead in request-
ing the change. They came with their chief villeins in the lead and
offered to pay forty shillings to be allowed to switch to primogeniture.[27]

Another form of protest against unusual services and tallages or
violations of old privileges was refusal to perform the required services. Manorial courts routinely recorded cases of people using hand
mills and refusing to take their grain to the lord's mill, or of people
failing to appear for work services or performing them poorly. On
some occasions these work strikes were well organized and a number of villeins put down their tools.[28] At Broughton in 1290 the
villeins under the leadership of the main villagers refused to do service because they had customarily received food with their boon
work and the abbot of Ramsey had stinted them.[29] The main village families were also the ones who had most of the work defaults
charged against them personally.[30]

Passive resistance and legal battles were only one type of confrontation between lord and peasant; there were also violent clashes.
Outright assassination of a lord was rare. First, because the clergy

and nobility travelled with a large group of retainers, it was difficult for a peasant to get close enough to strike. Second, the punishment for killing one's lord and master was the same as that for treason—drawing and hanging. Villagers could be sure that either the culprit or some of their innocent neighbors would be caught and punished for such a flagrant act against the social order. Nevertheless, the peasantry did sometimes ambush a particularly odious lord. Robert Warde of Burnham managed to kill his lord. Robert de Hoo of Compton, a shepherd, admitted that he and four other men lay in ambush at midnight for their lord, Thomas Goffe. As Sir Thomas came down the road from London they intercepted him at "la Knolle" in Windlesham and killed him with knives, swords and staffs.[31] These men were all punished with the prescribed torture. But Robert son of John le Taillour was acquitted by the jury because he killed his lord in self-defense. Lord Robert de la More attempted to run him down with a horse and lance but Robert was able to kill him first.[32]

Although peasants rarely murdered their lords, they frequently committed theft and burglary against them. In studying the crime patterns of the Ramsey Abbey villagers, I found that the abbot was a frequent victim of thefts committed by the highest status villeins. Acquisitiveness may not have been the sole motivation. In Broughton in 1294 John Gere, Thomas Gere, John son of Simon Crane and William son of John Roger were all tried and acquitted for burglary of the abbot's barn. The amount of grain stolen, two bushels worth only 15d, was hardly an attractive theft for four men who came from some of the wealthiest villein families in the village. It is possible that the men were stealing the quantity of grain that they thought was owed them for boon work. It was only four years previous that the general strike was held in Broughton over exactly this issue.[33] These men had long histories of work defaults to their names before the burglary.

Property crimes also reflected direct acts of revolt against the lords. Thomas de Burton of Thornton in Spalding was accused of breaking into a box belonging to Lord Thomas de Ros, lord of Melburn, and taking charters, muniments and other papers. Another man robbed John Skeet, bailiff of the Hundred of Depwade, of his records and rolls.[34]

Villagers resisted royal impositions through criminal means as well. The local assessors of Wiltshire taxes were refused cattle and other goods that they demanded. When they tried to take them one man assaulted them and they were forced to kill him in self-defense.[35] Two unwilling recruits for the war in Scotland killed the royal official who had recruited them.

> John son of Simon Robert of Cold Ashby, the constable, was found slain at Cold Ashby. He had a wound through the body made with a lance. The jury says that Richard son of William Clerk of Crick and John son of Richard of Ashby were enlisted to serve the king against the Scots at Northampton, and on their way, they came to Ashby, where they found the said John who had enlisted them. A quarrel ensued in which John was killed. The two assailants fled to the church of Ashby. The recruits of Northampton arrived and removed them from the church.[36]

Since the royal armies routinely recruited known felons to serve in the army in exchange for a pardon after a year's service, the two men were simply returned to their unit.

Peasants also occasionally engaged in organized acts of armed rebellion. The most famous case was the revolt of the villeins of Darnall and Over in 1336.[37] Before this armed attack on the abbot, there had been a violent history of conflict. Initially the villeins had gone in a body to see Sir Hugh de Fren, who was then the justiciar of Chester. They complained to him that they had formerly been free tenants by a charter granted by the king but that the abbot had violated this custom and had put them in confinement as if they were villeins and had even shackled them. After they had returned to their homes, the abbot sent out his servants, who rounded up the offenders and put them in fetters until they were willing to admit that they were in bondage and would do the services as previously.

The peasants, however, had given in only temporarily. They met again and "plotted at night to get their liberty by rebelling against the aforesaid abbot." They invented a ruse to send some of their members to the king. A group of them claimed that they were going on a pilgrimage to the shrine of St. Thomas of Hereford. Instead, they sought out the king, who was in northern England, and begged him to rectify their problems. Their pleas were interrupted when they were arrested on charges of robbery and put into Nottingham jail. They were found guilty as charged, but since the goods stolen were worth less than 12d, they were released. The charges may have been legitimate, but it is also possible that the abbot arranged to have them arrested. The monastic account of the revolt commented with a certain glee that the whole incident had cost the inhabitants of Over a great deal of money.

Even the imprisonment of their delegation did not deter the villeins. They presented a petition to the king and Parliament at Westminster complaining of the abbot's oppressions and saying that they could not return to their homes because of their dread of the abbot's actions.

Villein tempers were wearing thin by this time and they plotted to intercept the abbot on the highway in Rutland county. There was a skirmish in which the abbot's groom was killed and a number of people wounded. But with reinforcements from the local peasants, they were able to take the abbot prisoner. With the usual great faith that the peasants exhibited toward the king, they took the abbot to him. They got the reward that their naiveté deserved. The king released the abbot and imprisoned the bondmen. The king's justices did show a remarkable leniency toward the rebels, however. They were acquitted of the groom's death and were given a writ to the abbot directing him to return the lands and chattels of the rebels if he had seized them because of the groom's death.

The abbot, however, proved to be as oppressive as the bondmen had maintained and did not return their goods and land. The rebels were left with a choice of becoming landless wanderers or returning and submitting to the abbot. As a chronicler observed: "At length the bondmen, finding no other place in which they might be longer concealed, returned to the abbot their lord, submitting themselves and their goods to his grace, and the abbot put them all in fetters as his bondmen." Nor was he content to let the matter rest with winning his point; he also extracted a public humiliation. "And for many Sundays they stood in the choir, in the face of the convent, with bare heads and feet and they offered wax candles in token of subjection." His contempt for his serfs was similar to that of another abbot who told his chastised bondmen that they were to remember that they owned "nothing but their bellies."[38]

Most of the examples used so far in this paper have dealt with the thirteenth and early fourteenth centuries, but it would be interesting to know if these activities intensified leading up to the Great Revolt of 1381. The reduction of population resulting from recurrent visits of the Black Death did have an influence on popular unrest. First, plague was a powerful social leveller. The early fourteenth century had seen its share of misery, sickness, and death but these had all been related to famine conditions. Poor men starved to death but the rich did not. Plague, on the other hand, killed rich as well as poor. Second, as we have seen, peasants surviving the plague found that they could sell their labor at a high price. The customary services on the manors that had to be performed free began to look like intolerable burdens. Furthermore, land was now readily available for those who wanted to rent. The peasants were on the verge of improving their economic position but the lords and king seemed intent on hindering their success.

The Statute of Laborers was particularly hated and met with considerable resistence as the surviving justice of the peace rolls indicate. A preliminary study of the Lincolnshire rolls has shown that 37.5 percent of the cases coming before the justices of peace involved the new economic legislation while 32.5 percent dealt with felonies and 30 percent with trespasses. When labor offenses were analyzed, 26 percent were cases of breaking the compulsory service clause. This provision prohibited mobility of laborers and set idlers to work. An additional 25 percent of the cases involved accusations of taking excess wages. Not only were laborers breaking the laws, but craftsmen were also raising the prices on goods on which they expended their labor. Thus 27 percent of the economic offenses were for charging excessive prices. In sharp contrast, few employers were prosecuted for the clauses against abducting servants or giving excess wages—6 percent and 2 percent respectively. The resentment against the new law also showed up in cases where a person was indicted for both a labor offense and for resisting officials. Those facing these double charges accounted for 9 percent of the labor cases.[39] Langland's observations were very keen when he wrote:

> And so it is nowadays—the labourer is angry unless he gets high wages, and he curses the day that he was ever born a workman.... But he blames God, and murmurs against Reason, and curses the king and his Council for making Statutes on purpose to plague the workman![40]

The manorial records as well show an increasing revolt of villeins against performing labor services. On the manor of Hollywell-cum-Needingworth there were an average of four labor derelictions a year between 1288 and 1339. From 1353 to 1403 there were an average of fourteen a year. The highest years were in 1353 with twenty-six labor deficiencies, 1372 with thirty-two, 1378 with twenty-four, and 1386 with twenty-six. Not only were the villeins failing to turn up for work or doing it inadequately, they were more brazen about allowing their cattle to wander in demesne land.[41]

The number of tenants who organized themselves to resist their lords through local revolt or appeals to law might also have increased. At least the language reporting peasant resistance showed an awareness of the greater degree of peasant organization. A report on Strixton manor in Northamptonshire complained that the peasants "confederated themselves in conventicles, and took an oath to resist lord and bailiff, and to refuse their due custom and service."[42] The sources for studying local revolts, however, are unsystematic so that it is difficult to have a quantitative measure of increased rebellion.

Contemporaries, however, perceived that there was an increase and in 1377 a petition in Commons complained that:

> the villeins and tenants of land in villeinage, who owe services and customs to the lords for various reasons and within various lordships, both ecclesiastical and secular, have (through the advice, procurement, maintenance and abetting of certain persons) purchased in the king's court for their own profit exemplifications from the Book of Domesday — concerning those manors and vills where these villeins and tenants live.

The petition went on to claim that the peasants misinterpreted the exemplifications and withdrew the customs and services due to their lords, claiming that they were free from such exactions because they were part of ancient royal demesne. The crown replied that the exemplifications from the Domesday Book could not be used either to claim personal freedom or to release villeins from customary services.[43]

The second part of the petition was even more ominous. It pointed out that the villeins "have refused to allow the officials of the lords to distrain them for the said customs and services; and have made confederation and alliance together to resist the lords and their officials by force, so that each will aid the other whenever they are distrained for any reason." The peasant resistance was made to sound like a well-organized conspiracy charging that the peasants had "collected large sums of money among themselves to meet their costs and expenses." Finally, the petition predicted that either war would break out or that the villeins would collude with a foreign enemy for an invasion. The king assured the lords and commons in an ordinance that any who "feel themselves aggrieved shall have special commissions of inquiry appointed under the Great Seal."[44]

The king and his lords had reason for a sense of urgency in their actions in 1377–1378. For the years between 1341 and 1377 R. H. Tillotson found evidence for only four appeals to the Domesday Book on the part of the peasantry, but from March to August of 1377 there were twenty such exemplifications requested. While only one of these succeeded, it was not irrational to see a conspiracy in the number of requests. The evidence indicates that when the villagers met regionally for the view of frankpledge in 1377 they had exchanged ideas about how the exemplifications could work in their favor. Village after village in Wiltshire and Hampshire requested exemplifications and generally abandoned their labor services. The local landlords had to request the Council to direct the sheriff to put down these sporadic revolts. Within three weeks the villagers of Surrey began to ask for exemplifications. It was this rash of activity in the south that led to the Ordinance of 1377.[45] Surprisingly, there was no rush on the part of the nobility to use the oyer and terminer commissions for aid against the rebellious villagers in 1378. The Patent Rolls indicate only ten commissions issued under the terms of the Ordinance. After 1378 the commissions are not used again until the end of Richard II's reign.[46]

Tillotson is probably correct in suggesting that the Ordinance of 1377 was the counterpart of the Statute of Laborers. While the Statute controlled wages and free movement of the peasants, the Ordinance tried to keep intact the old servile dues of villeinage.[47]

What made the Great Revolt of 1381 different from the previous rebellions? Oman concluded that "the only thing that was new in 1381 was that the troubles were not confined to individual manors, but suddenly spread over half the realm."[48] The evidence we have presented tends to support this conclusion, for the acts of violence committed against the lords and royal officials were of the same sort and for the same reasons as before.

The revolt started in Brentwood in Essex when one of the new tax commissioners arrived to reassess the population for the poll tax. The villagers were prepared for him. When he summoned the Fobbing men before him, they arrived 100 strong with reinforcements from surrounding villages. In rude language they informed him that they would pay not a penny more. When he directed his sergeants to arrest the spokesmen, the peasants set upon the royal officials and stoned them out of town. Other tax collectors lost their lives to similar organized resistance.

As the revolt spread, the peasants broke into muniment rooms across the country and destroyed records of villeinage. They murdered those lords, lay and ecclesiastical, and royal officials who were so unfortunate as to fall into their hands. They looted manors and town houses of their oppressors. The form of retribution was the same as before, but on a larger scale.

As in the court cases and the earlier revolts, the king was looked to as the one person who would understand the peasants' plight and rectify the wrongs they had suffered for so long. Hence they converged on London, killed the king's councilors who were responsible for the poll tax, and sought a direct audience with their monarch. After he had granted them an interview at Mile End, they requested that all of those oppressions and restrictions that they had been fighting for centuries should at last be removed. Richard, surrounded by an unruly mob, agreed to end serfdom, make everyone a free tenant paying only 4d annually per acre to his lord, and remove restrictions on buying and selling. Many people trusted the hastily drawn-up royal charters and departed feeling that they had gained their ends at the hands of a benevolent king.[49] The charters were later repudiated by statute because they were issued under duress. But the king showed the same sort of restraint in punishing rebels that had been shown previously toward the tenants of Darnall and Over and to the Cellarer family. While many people were indicted after the revolt, relatively few were hanged.

The leadership of the revolt was chosen from the group that had led earlier revolts or had taken the communities' cases to royal courts. They were the prominent villagers in their region, rather than being the most downtrodden of the peasantry. Some of the leaders, such as Sir Roger Bacon and Sir Thomas Cornerd, were even from the gentry ranks.

Some aspects of the revolt, however, reflect more than a mere increase in the magnitude of rebellion. First, the revolt spread too quickly in most areas to have been simply a spontaneous rising. In 1377 the Commons claimed that the peasants had been organizing and even had common treasuries. There is no reason to assume that the organization had gone far enough to have premeditated the revolt, but it might have gone far enough to respond quickly when the revolt broke out. Furthermore, the revolt in the southeast, at least, showed signs of being more disciplined than in some of the other areas.

During the 1370s and 1380s when the southeastern coast had been attacked repeatedly by French raiding parties, the king and local nobles had abandoned the area and its people. The only magnate in the area that fought with the peasant militia was the abbot of Battle Abbey. When the revolt broke out in 1381 the first target of the men of Sussex was the earl of Arundel's castle at Lewes. Joining forces with the men from Kent they burnt Gaunt's Savoy Palace. Battle Abbey and its heroic abbot were left untouched. The march on London from Kent and Sussex was in the nature of the hundred levies of the militia. The peasants had become soldiers to defend the realm, and they used their knowledge to revolt against the government.[50]

In addition to military organization, the villagers and townsmen had long-established parish gilds that served not only religious and convivial functions, but also groomed the community political leaders. People with local political ambitions joined the most prestigious parish gild.[51] The gilds could have provided the leadership for local revolts and also a network for communicating local plans for revolt to a region. In one case, at least, the gild network has been documented. After the revolt in St. Albans, the abbot suppressed the gilds of St. Alban, St. John the Baptist, and Holy Trinity because their members had provided leaders and rioters for the revolt. They were only allowed to reorganize years later under the oath that they would not be politically subversive. In the course of the revolt they had reached the countryside surrounding St. Albans by sending out messengers to the gild leaders of the hinterland.[52] In 1389 the king requested that all parish gilds report the contents of their charters and the amount of their assets to the crown. The reasons for this request are unknown since the roll of Parliament for that year is lost. Some of the gilds obviously assumed that they might be suspect and assured the king that there was nothing political about their organization.[53]

The revolt of 1381 temporarily exhausted peasant protest, but four years later and into the fifteenth century cases appealing to the Domesday Book and local revolts continued to be reported.[54]

Major revolutionary changes, however, were not brought about by violence, strikes, and legal battles but by social and economic change. The increased economic opportunities made available by depopulation brought increased mobility and a greater differentiation of wealth and status among the peasantry. The cohesion of the village communities that had made revolt possible began to erode. J. Ambrose Raftis has shown that following the Black Death in Upton the old power structure of the village began to break up. The land was increasingly held by a few wealthy and powerful villagers, sometimes newcomers rather than members of the old village elite.[55] The evidence of the changes appeared sooner in Upton than in many other communities, but by the early fifteenth century the trend was apparent. Landlords found that even with repressive labor legislation they could not keep wages down or prevent their tenants from refusing to work on the demesne. By the first quarter of the fifteenth century direct farming of the demesne was generally abandoned and the land was rented to entrepreneurs and wealthy peasants. Those peasants who acquired extensive lands ceased to identify with the other villagers and came to form the new social class of yeomen. As yeomen they had more in common with the gentry than with fellow villagers. Communities were thus deprived of their leadership and were less likely to have joint causes or to make common complaints.

Because lords were no longer farming their demesne, they had less need for traditional labor services and found that they could make more money by manumitting their villeins than by keeping them on the manor. The manumission of villeins increased their mobility and removed the need for complaints about unpaid services.[56] Those peasants remaining in the villages gradually ceased to pay the money that was owed in lieu of services. They were willing to pay a just rent for the land, but did not want to pay an annual due that reminded them of villein status.[57]

Royal oppressions likewise ceased to be as severe in the fifteenth century. The crown abandoned the poll tax and actually taxed far less frequently. Although the Statute of Laborers remained in force, it became increasingly difficult to regulate the more mobile labor force.

It has frequently been said that the Great Revolt of 1381 accomplished nothing, and yet perceptible change in attitude toward the problems of the peasantry is discernible. When Parliament met in December of 1381 to revoke the charters of manumission and generally hold a post mortem on the recent events, Sir Richard de Waldegrave, who was speaker of Commons, protested that the "mean commons" were not solely to blame for the revolt. He and other members admonished the government for corruption. They complained that, because the nobles kept armed households, law and justice were impossible to obtain. Purveyances had despoiled and destroyed peasants and the subsidies and tallages levied on them had brought the poor commons "to great wretchedness and misery, more than they ever were before." Foreign enemies had invaded the kingdom with robbery and pillage and yet the king had done nothing to protect his poor subjects. "The said poor commons, who once used to live in all honour and prosperity, can no longer endure in any way." It was the outrages of the lords and kings that made the "said poor commons feel so hardly oppressed and caused the said mean commons to rise and commit the mischief they did in the said riot."[58]

Political poetry and polemical writings also changed. The fourteenth century produced little protest literature about the condition of the peasantry, but following the revolt there is a rich variety of poems showing both lower class self-confidence and upper class concern for the plight of the poor commons. Behind the poets' concern for the commons was the fear that unless they were cared for, they would rise in revolt once again.[59] But as they wrote, the conditions that incited the Great Revolt were disappearing. The struggle of the fifteenth century increasingly centered not on burdensome labor services on the land but on losing traditional rights to the land to enclosures.

Notes

1. Ester Boserup, *Women's Role in Economic Development* (London, 1970).
2. Edgar Powell, *The Rising in East Anglia in 1381* (Cambridge, 1896); A. Réville, *Le soulèvement des travailleurs d'Angleterre en 1381*, ed. Charles Petit-Dutaillis (Paris, 1898); Charles Oman, *The Great Revolt of 1381*, new edition ed. E. B. Fryde (Oxford, 1969).
3. R. H. Hilton, *Bond Men Made Free; Medieval Peasant Movements and the English Rising of 1381* (London, 1973) and "Peasant Movements in England before 1381" in *Essays in Economic History*, ed. E. M. Carus-Wilson (London, 1962), pp. 73–90.
4. *Collections for a History of Staffordshire*, The William Salt Archaeological Society, vol. 16 (1895), p. 17. Taken from Chester Plea Roll no. 68.
5. Hilton, *Bond Men Made Free*, pp. 88–90.
6. Public Record Office (hereafter P. R. O.), Just. 2/106 m. 1.
7. Harold Schneebeck, "The Law of Felony in Medieval England from the Accession of Edward I until the Mid-fourteenth Century" (Ph. D. diss., University of Iowa, 1973), pp. 478–79.
8. *Bedfordshire Coroners' Rolls*, ed. and trans. R. F. Hunnisett, Bedfordshire Record Society, vol. 41 (1960), p. 82.
9. Hilton, *Bond Men Made Free*, pp. 151–52. For a discussion of how the peasants manipulated the judicial system, see Barbara A. Hanawalt "Community Conflict and Social Control: Crime in the Ramsey Abbey Villages," *Mediaeval Studies* 39 (1977): 402–23.
10. J. R. Maddicott, *The English Peasantry and the Demands of the Crown*, Past and Present Society, Supplement 1 (1975).
11. Ibid., pp. 11–12.
12. Edmund B. Fryde, "English Parliament and the Peasants' Revolt of 1381," in *Liber Memorialis Georges de Lagarde*, International Commission for the History of Representative and Parliamentary Institutions, vol. 38 (1968), p. 83.
13. Ibid., pp. 75–78.
14. Ibid., pp. 78–81.
15. Ibid., pp. 84–85.
16. Maddicott, *The English Peasantry*, pp. 15–16.
17. Ibid., pp. 19–27.
18. Ibid., pp. 30–31.
19. Ibid., pp. 35–45. The drain of warfare on the coastal regions has received close attention in an article by Eleanor Searle and Robert Burghart, "The Defense of England and the Peasants' Revolt," *Viator* 3 (1972): 365–88.
20. Berthan H. Putnam, *The Enforcement of the Statute of Labourers during the First Decade after the Black Death, 1349–1359,* Columbia University Studies in History, Economics and Public Law, vol. 32, (1908).
21. Austin Land Poole, *Obligations of Society in the Twelfth and Thirteenth Centuries* (Oxford, 1946), pp. 30–34 for examples.
22. Helen Maud Cam., *Liberties and Communities in Medieval England* (Cambridge, 1944), pp. 131–32. Hilton also cites cases in "Peasant Movements," p. 79.

23. Marjorie J. O. Kennedy, "Resourceful Villeins: the Cellarer Family of Wawne in Holderness," *Yorkshire Archaeological Journal* 48 (1976): 109–16.

24. George Homans, *English Villagers of the Thirteenth Century* (New York, 1941), pp. 277–84.

25. Hilton, "Peasant Movements in England," p. 81.

26. J. F. Nichols, "An Early Fourteenth Century Petition from the Tenants of Bocking to their Manorial Lord," *Economic History Review* 2 (1929/30): 300–307.

27. *Chertsey Abbey Court Rolls Abstract,* ed. and trans. Elsie Toms, Surrey Record Society, vol. 21 (part one, 1937), p. xiii.

28. Hilton, "Peasant Movements in England," p. 82.

29. Edward J. Britton, "Broughton 1288–1340: A Mediaeval Village Community," (Ph. D. diss., University of Toronto, 1973), pp. 370–72.

30. Edwin B. DeWindt, *Land and People in Holywell-cum-Needingworth* (Toronto, 1972), pp. 268–69.

31. P. R. O., Just. 3/49/1 m. 50, 3/129 m. 58.

32. P. R. O., Just. 3/214/4 m. 9.

33. P. R. O., Just. 3/94 m. 9d.

34. P. R. O., Just. 3/169 m. 27, 3/175 m. 2.

35. P. R. O., Just. 2/195 m. 10.

36. P. R. O., Just. 2/109 m. 1.

37. G. G. Coulton, *The Medieval Village* (Cambridge, 1925), pp. 132–35.

38. Ibid., p. 131.

39. Madonna Hettinger of Hamilton College kindly supplied these figures to me from her dissertation in progress.

40. William Langland, *Piers the Ploughman,* trans. J. F. Goodridge (Harmondsworth, UK, 1959), p. 90.

41. DeWindt, *Land and People,* pp. 268–69.

42. Oman, *The Great Revolt,* p. 10.

43. *Rot. Parl.* 3:21–22. Translations taken from R. B. Dobson, *The Peasants' Revolt of 1381* (London, 1970), pp. 76–78.

44. Ibid.

45. R. H. Tillotson, "Peasant Unrest in England of Richard II," *Historical Studies* 16 (1974): 3–6.

46. Ibid., p. 7.

47. Ibid., p. 16.

48. Oman, *The Great Revolt,* p. 12.

49. Ibid., p. 64.

50. Searle and Burghart, "Defense of England," pp. 382–87.

51. C. Phythian-Adams, *Desolation of a City: Coventry and the Urban Crisis of the Late Middle Ages* (Cambridge, 1979), pp. 119–21.

52. *Victoria County History: Hertfordshire,* ed. William Page, 2 (1908): 48 and 4 (1928): 204–307.

53. For a publication of the gild returns see Toulmin Smith and Lucy Toulmin Smith, eds., *English Gilds: The Original Ordinances of More than 100 English Gilds,* Early English Texts Society, o.s. vol. 40 (1870).

54. Tillotson, "Peasant Unrest," p. 9–10. There were twenty commissions of Oyer and Terminer from 1385 to 1399.

55. J. Ambrose Raftis, "Changes in an English Village after the Black Death," *Mediaeval Studies* 29 (1967): 158–77.

56. Frances G. Davenport, "The Decay of Villeinage in East Anglia," in *Essays in Economic History*, ed. E. M. Carus-Wilson (London, 1962), pp. 112–124.

57. R. H. Hilton, *The English Peasantry in the Later Middle Ages* (Oxford, 1975), p. 65.

58. Dobson, *The Peasants' Revolt of 1381*, pp. 330–31.

59. V. J. Scattergood, *Politics and Poetry in the Fifteenth Century* (London, 1971), pp. 351–60. See also Rossell Hope Robbins, "Dissent in Middle English Literature: The Spirit of (Thirteen) Seventy-six," *Medievalia et Humanistica* (1976): 25–51.

Chaucer and the Economic and Social Consequences of the Plague

D. W. Robertson, Jr.

I.

I HOPE YOU WILL PARDON ME if in this lecture I devote more attention to background than to the work of Chaucer, which I should much prefer to discuss. Again, you may notice a certain skepticism on my part concerning the topic announced in the title. The series of plagues that struck England during Chaucer's lifetime undoubtedly contributed to social change and to social unrest, but the effects of disease are difficult to isolate from those of other kinds of hardship, and it is also true that they might have been very different in a differently structured society with other means of response and other attitudes. Moreover, a change in ways of doing things in one area of human activity is likely to have repercussions in other areas and to produce situations that are in themselves, regardless of their origins, productive of further changes and developments. It may help to remind ourselves of what some of the "other kinds of hardship" were, and we are fortunately able to do so from a fourteenth-century point of view. In the jubilee address Edward III prepared to be read in Parliament, for he was too ill to attend himself, in the fiftieth year of his reign (1377), the king, who was about to announce a comprehensive pardon for various offenses and debts, spoke of "the great charges and losses which the said people [his subjects] have had and suffered in times past, as well as by the wars, and otherwise by the pestilence of the people, murrain of beasts, and the fruits of the land commonly failed by evil years in times past, whereof our Sovereign Lord the King hath great compassion...."[1] It is noteworthy that the king mentioned "the wars" first, before going on to mention what might be called in modern legal parlance "acts of God," although it is true that a great many people, including King Edward, regarded all of the things he mentioned as being the providential consequences of sin.[2] Warfare was something for which Edward as king exercised primary responsibility, and after the resumption of the war with France in 1368 England did not fare very well. In addition to human losses in the field through military action or disease, war entailed onerous taxation, purveyance on a large scale, sometimes extortionate, the activation of commissioners of array who were not always honest, and widespread subjection to the misbehavior of troops either moving toward ports of departure or awaiting departure in the areas of ports. Again, returned soldiers often became robbers instead of settling down to honest labor. In fact, it was one of the first duties of the justices of the peace when they were established to seize and arrest such all persons who could be found.[3] In some coastal regions and in the Scottish border area many persons suffered from the ravages of enemy raiders, and commercial shipping was frequently impeded. During the following reign under Richard, England's fortunes in warfare steadily declined. Partly as a result of taxation that seemed ineffectual, partly as a result of coastal raids, and partly as a result of other factors, for some of which the government was responsible, a revolt broke out in 1381. By 1386 the country was faced by an enormous hostile invasion fleet and by simultaneous threats from the north and the south. The court had been disrupted into factions, the king was threatened with deposition, and a civil uprising led to the drastic actions of the Merciless Parliament. When it was not waged effectively war could lead to attacks on English ports and severe disruptions in trade, necessary to the welfare of all social ranks.[4]

During the last years of his reign Edward did not exercise very firm control of his government either in war[5] or in matters of routine administration, although he did not mention this fact in the preamble to his jubilee pardon. But corruption or highhanded action could and did give rise to unrest. The king had been warned about these matters early in his reign, first by Archbishop Mepham, who observed that the illegal and extortionate behavior of household purveyors might lead to rebellion,[6] and then by Archbishop Stratford who threatened to excommunicate royal officers who at Edward's behest had imprisoned a number of persons without due process in violation of the Great Charter.[7] However, Edward issued a series of statutes to control purveyors for royal or baronial households, the most comprehensive of which in 1362 would have solved the problem if it had been faithfully enforced.[8] The failure of his early efforts to buy allies abroad also taught him the dangers of excessive taxation. It must be said in his favor that he sought to control the actions of sheriffs and bailiffs. A statute of 1340 (14 Ed III 1.7)[9] demanded that sheriffs be appointed for only one year, and that each have only one bailiff errant or "outrider"; for "outriders," it was said, had "notoriously destroyed the people." When Chaucer called his monk, probably an external cellarer, an "outrider" he was using pejorative language suggestive of extortion.[10] In 1354 (28 Ed III 7)[11] it was stipulated that no sheriff could succeed himself. And in 1368 (42 Ed III 9)[12] it was decreed that estreats (or extracts from exchequer rolls sent to the sheriff so that he could collect fines and amercements) be clearly marked to identify their purposes and that they be sealed and totted in the presence of the debtor upon payment so that they could not be used twice for the same fine. Finally in 1372[13] sheriffs were forbidden to act as members of Parliament, along with lawyers doing business for the king. In addition to extortionate sheriffs and bailiffs the men of the shires had to contend with unscrupulous and greedy escheators.[14] A statute of 1360 (34 Ed III 12)[15] stipulated that escheators who seized land for alleged treason in deceased ancestors should warn their victims first with writs of *scire facias* so that they might present an answer on a given day, that the inquests held by escheators should be made before "good people of good fame," in the counties, and that inquests be indentured between the escheators and the juries so that the presentations of escheators could be verified. Further, tenants whose lands were seized because they had alienated without royal license, or were said to be heirs within age, could be heard at King's Bench if they objected. The abuses indicated are clear enough.

Perhaps more important were the remedies Edward decreed for abuses in the administration of justice, especially his great Ordinance for the Justices of 1346,[16] designed to prevent maintenance and procurement. If it had been enforced a great many miseries might have been avoided. The king, calling attention to the abuses just mentioned, said that he was "greatly moved of conscience in this matter," so that as much "for the pleasure of God and the ease and quietness of our subjects, as to save our conscience, and to save and keep our said oath, we have ordained the things following." I shall summarize them briefly:

1. All justices should treat rich and poor alike with no regard

to persons (a scriptural principle, incidentally[17]) and should dis-
regard "any letters or commandment" either from the king or anyone else that might impede equal right, and should report any such
letters to the king and Council.

2. Justices should take no fees or robes from anyone except the
king, and no gifts beyond food and drink of small value.

3. They should give no counsel to anyone, great or small, in matters involving the king (or actions *contra pacem*, felonies, or cases
involving lands held by tenants in chief).

4. The barons of the exchequer should treat rich and poor alike
and avoid delays.

5. Justices of assize and jail delivery should take an oath to observe the ordinance.

6. No one in the royal household should maintain the cause of
another, and each should keep the ordinance.

7. All great men should eliminate from their households fees and
robes for "bearers and maintainers," who were to be brought before the king and his council.

8. The justices of assize were instructed to "inquire of sheriffs,
escheators, bailiffs of franchises, and of their under ministers, and
also of maintainers, common embracers, and jurors in the country" concerning the "gifts, rewards, and other profits which the said
ministers do take of the people to execute their office, and that which
pertaineth to their office, and of making array of panels [one of
the chief duties of the sheriff], putting in the same suspect jurors,
and of evil fame; and of the fact that maintainers, embracers, and
jurors do take rewards against the parties,[18] whereby losses do
come daily to the people...."

9. Such persons were to be punished "as law and reason requires"
both at the suit of the king and the suit of the parties, and the
chancellor and the treasurer should be alerted to hear complaints.

This Ordinance was repeated as a statute in 1384 (8 R II 3),[19]
with the stipulation that those justices found guilty lose their offices, but it was repealed in the following year as being "too severe." An effort to revive it in 1386 when Chaucer was attending
Parliament failed.

Edward reinforced his Ordinance in 1357 in a statute against
champerty (31 Ed III 4.10).[20] In effect this pointed out that sergeants of the law and even court clerks act as maintainers, conniv-
ing with third persons to bring false suit against landholders to gain

their lands, thus acquiring such lands at little or no cost to themselves. And in 1360 (34 Ed III 7–8)[21] a statute made it possible for even the poor, who could not pay a fine, to obtain a writ of attaint against a juror alleged to have taken anything to reach his verdict. In the same year the king established the justices of the peace in the counties[22] to "determine at the king's suit all manner of felonies and trespasses," stipulating that the justices assigned "be named by the court and not by the party," thus seeking to eliminate in part the evil of allowing those who brought suit to name their own justices whose actions they might control. These justices became responsible for enforcing the Statute of Laborers, to which I shall return in a moment, in 1368. Finally, Edward issued a series of statutes seeking to control the easy granting of pardons for felonies.[23]

Unfortunately, this considerable body of legislation in so far as it was designed to control corruption and maintenance was largely disregarded. If anything, maintenance of one kind or another increased, and the situation did not improve during the reign of Richard II, who seemed considerably less concerned about corruption than his predecessor, especially when he could use it to further his own ends. Sheriffs were sometimes almost forced to use extortion to collect the farm of the counties, impoverished by war or pestilence, or by the granting of hundreds to private parties; and officials of all kinds, both lay and ecclesiastic, enriched themselves through their offices. Extortion among coroners,[24] bailiffs of hundreds, and archdeacons,[25] became commonplace. As organizations, both lay and ecclesiastic, became more efficient and centralized, they tended at the same time to become more corrupt. Centralization also produced what has been called "bastard feudalism," although I do not think that "feudalism," much less "bastard feudalism," is a very useful term.[26] In this connection some historians like to dwell on the evil consequences of the statute *quia emptores* issued by Edward I in 1290,[27] which in effect put an end to subinfeudation in fee simple, even though its purpose was to maintain ties between lord and tenant. The popularity of final concords, which gave free tenants of all kinds some of the convenience associated with transactions in borough courts, for transfers of land, rents, leases, and other holdings that were recorded as "feet of fines" and kept as central records, contributed further to centralization. It was quite natural that legal manipulation of one kind or another should have been used to supplement force.[28]

In the first Parliament of Richard II, memorable for John of Gaunt's spirited defense of his integrity, further statutes, for which the boy king was of course not responsible, were issued against maintenance. After a preliminary general decree on the subject, widespread discontent among serfs was attributed to maintainers who had "taken hire and profit of the said villeins and landtenants" to provide them with "certain exemplifications made out of the Book of Domesday" to prove that they did not owe their "services and customs" (1 R II 6).[29] As a result of their activities tenants were said to have formed confederacies to resist their lords, setting "an evil example to others to begin such riots." It is clear that what is known rather inaccurately[30] as "The Peasants' Revolt" was already getting under way in agricultural communities, and that it was being stimulated by unscrupulous persons with some literate competence for their own profit. The commons expressed a justified fear of "greater mischiefs, which God forbid, throughout the realm." Judicial inquiries were instituted to imprison the rebels and "their counsellors, procurers, maintainers, and abettors." This was followed by a statute (c. 7) against "persons of small revenue of land" who made confederacies with liveries of hats or other liveries and agreed to maintain one another in quarrels "reasonable or unreasonable." Another decree forbade enfeoffments of disputed land or other tenures to great men for maintenance. Other reform measures included one against clerks of the exchequer who connived to issue second writs for debts already paid (c. 5), and (c. 11) against the reinstatement of sheriffs within three years.[31] The commons had complained that sheriffs arrested people for homicide in their tourns without due process and held them in prison for high ransoms.[32] For their part some sheriffs complained that they could not collect the farm of the counties. The sheriff of Exeter and Hertford said that he had lost £100 a year, and that since the last pestilence the loss had been even greater.[33] Temporary remedies were supplied in the form of allowances granted to some sheriffs in succeeding years, but a solution to the problem did not appear until the first year of Henry IV, who realized that sheriffs could not pay the long-established farms "without doing extortion" (1 H IV 11).[34]

In their convocation the clergy in this first year of Richard's reign

drew up complaints against the extravagances of the royal household, a traditional difficulty that was to become worse in the future, against the illegal seizure of clergymen by the officers of the
Marshalsea, and against buyers and purveyors who, in spite of the
warnings of Archbishop Mepham and King Edward's subsequent
legislation, continued to seize goods. They were also burdened,
they said, by the visits of sheriffs and their families to monasteries
and priories, which caused heavy expense.[35] Again, they complained that laymen were forcibly oppressing ecclesiastical courts
and preventing their functioning. For their part the commons asked
that no "dean, official, archdeacon, or other curates" take money
for the correction of sin but instead administer spiritual penances,
that cures of souls are let to farm like lands and tenements in lay
fee "for the increase from year to year," and complained further
that curates take exorbitant fees for wills.[36] The contribution of
corruption in ecclesiastical courts together with the effects of im-
poverishment of the clergy in many parishes and the abandonment
of many chapels as a result of pestilence have often been neglected
as causes of social unrest. It is quite obvious that King Edward,
who had for some years left governmental responsibilities to others,
died at a time when his realm was in considerable disarray, har-
rassed by enemies abroad, and demoralized in its domestic functions by greed among both laymen and ecclesiastics. What the author of *Piers Plowman* called "Lady Meed," or what Chaucer in the
Pardoner's Tale called *cupiditas,* seemed to be the true queen of the
commonwealth.

This impression is strengthened if we glance briefly at parliamentary activity during the years immediately preceding the outbreak
of large-scale revolt. In the second year of Richard's reign there
was a complaint about extortionate summoners, a kind of anticipa-
tion of Chaucer's *Friar's Tale.* They were said to make summons
out of malice, extorting money from the poor, or summoning them
to distant places, making them pay fines they called "the bishop's
alms."[37] There was also a complaint that agricultural workers had
gone to vills, boroughs, and towns to become artificers, mariners,
or clerks, so that husbandry was difficult to maintain.[38] This difficulty, which may be attributed in part to the effects of pestilence,
and in part to the growth of industries,[39] was one that persisted
throughout the century, as the rolls of the justices of the peace reveal. A statute was passed against mariners, who after having been

arrested and retained for the king's service, fled with their wages, sometimes having bribed sergeants at arms or masters of ships.[40] Another sought to punish those who spread false news and "horrible false lies" about prelates, dukes, earls, barons, and great men of the realm;[41] many such tales were spread about in the revolt soon to come, and it is quite probable that the process had already begun. Finally, it was agreed that no sheriff could be a justice of the peace.[42]

In the following year the commons of Norfolk, Suffolk, Kent, Surrey, Hampshire, Dorset, Devonshire, and Cornwall complained "that they and their houses are robbed and destroyed and wasted by armed men, archers and others passing in the service of the king and remaining a long time."[43] The commons of Northumberland were troubled by "mischiefs and damages" not only from the pestilence but from the Scots, so that they asked for wardens and garrisons to protect them.[44] The men of Staffordshire, Shropshire, Warwickshire, Hereford, and York asked relief from "devastation, rape, and mayhem" committed by bands of men from Chester, where a large area was a secular sanctuary protecting violent men.[45] Meanwhile, royal officers were still impeding justice. A petition complained that escheators suddenly disinherit and oust men from their lands and tenements who are delayed in their pursuit of justice either by force, by protection, or by other delays.[46] There was a strong complaint about benefices granted to aliens, sometimes "utter enemies of the king," who neglected to keep churches in repair, neglected divine service, and diminished reverence for the Church.[47] In response justices of the peace were given power to hear and determine concerning homicide, extortion, riding armed or in routs, lying in wait to commit mayhem or murder, and wearing livery of hats and other liveries for maitenance. The justices themselves were to be elected by the most sufficient knights and squires from each county, or by those then in Parliament, and to be paid in proportion to their rank. They were to meet four times a year or more often if necessary, and each justice was to take an oath "to do full right to all, to the poor as well as to the rich," and to avoid delays for benefits, promises, or "any articifice or stratagem whatsoever."[48] All this was perhaps a little late. In the following year there was a petition for better protection of the coasts, for the balingers of Normandy and other enemies were making great damages on the coasts, both in the north and in the south.[49]

It is obvious that there was considerable unrest throughout the realm before the revolt of 1381. The poll tax of 1380, as Sir Goronwy Edwards has recently explained, was a reasonable effort to avoid the inequities of the traditional tax of a fifteenth and a tenth, which was based on quotas established for each township and borough in 1344. During the intervening years some townships and boroughs had prospered while others had become impoverished. A tax to be collected in two installments based on an average of three groats per person, with the weak paying less and the strong more, seemed equitable and bearable.[50] However, when the initial proceeds collected in January seemed inadequate, the government ordered an inspection in March to check on the first collection, and this was sometimes regarded as a new tax without parliamentary consent. In any event, it precipitated riotous revolt,[51] by no means confined to peasants. The famous address to Parliament on the causes of the revolt by Sir Richard Waldgrave becomes much more understandable, I believe, in the light of the situation we have just been considering. He attributed the outbreak to "the government of the realm" which, he said, would be "lost and destroyed forever" if suitable remedies were not applied. Specifically, he called attention to the "outrageous numbers of familiars" in the royal household, in the chancery, king's bench, common bench, and exchequer. The implication of this statement was that there was widespread extravagance and corruption in the administration of justice, the chief function of the medieval king. He went on to elaborate by saying that there were "outrageous numbers" of embracers and maintainers "who are like kings in the country, so that right and loyalty are hardly made to anyone." Returning to the household, he said that the commons are "pillaged and destroyed" by purveyors for the household of the king and of others. They are distressed by "subsidies and tallages," and oppressed by "the ministers of the king and the lords of the realm," and especially by maintainers. Moreover, great treasures are levied for defense, but the commons, far from being defended, are "burned, robbed, and pillaged" by land and sea by enemies. These outrages and others, he concluded, had caused the lesser commons to revolt.[52]

Unfortunately, this address did not result in widespread reforms. In 1382 the commons said that there was not a bailiff in the counties who did not summon many good men for extortion.[53] There were complaints about rioters from Chester in 1382, 1384, 1390, and 1393.[54] A demand that justices of both benches treat rich and poor alike, and that the justices of the peace apprehend vagrants, thieves, and robbers was made in 1383, and a statute was issued against riding armed.[55] As one reads the parliamentary petitions of Richard's reign it becomes evident that Richard did little to enforce the reforming legislation of his predecessor, or even that of the early years of his own reign. In 1385 his chancellor failed to implement a series of reforms endorsed in Parliament, and in 1397 Richard accused a member of Parliament of treason for criticizing the extravagances of his household. Sir Richard Waldgrave's concern for the future was realized in 1386, when the king was threatened with deposition, and in the acts of the Merciless Parliament. The domestic grievances of which Waldgrave spoke, especially that concerning "the outrageous numbers of familiars" in the government, were grievous to the lords as well as to the commons, and it is not surprising that Richard, who became fearful of his own people, was ultimately deposed.

II

Sir Richard said nothing about "the pestilence of the people, murrain of beasts, and the fruits of the land commonly failed in evil years." I shall not dwell on the subjects of murrains or bad years, but both probably stimulated corruption among officials. Mercifully, there were no direct taxes between 1361 and 1370, during years of peace, but this respite was spoiled not only by pestilence in 1360 and 1361, but by murrain, drought, and by a devastating storm in Cornwall. As Barbara Hanawalt has shown,[56] there was a correlation between crime and high wheat prices during the years before the great pestilence, and there is no reason to suppose that this correlation did not continue.[57] The early sixties, when prices were high, certainly witnessed a rise in crime generally.[58] Again, in 1389 there were devastating floods that moved the king to forbid exports of grain and to forgive the customs on imported grain in 1391. But these moves brought prices so low in 1394 that the poor could not pay their rents.[59] Similar dislocations resulted from pestilence. However, I shall not pursue here the chronology of fourteenth-century pestilences, nor discuss the controversial question of the various diseases involved or the mortality rates from

each. Nor shall I describe in detail their effects on agricultural communities that have been described so well by Father Raftis and his
students especially.

The response of the government to the great pestilence was to
issue the Ordinance of Laborers,[60] soon to be followed by the Statute (25 Ed III 2,3).[61] The Ordinance began by calling attention
to the fact that after the pestilence servants took advantage of the
scarcity of labor and demanded "excessive wages," or even decided
to beg in idleness. It was decreed that anyone under the age of 60,
free or bond, without employment could be made to serve at the
rate usual in 1346 and 1347, or in the five or six "common years"
previously, on pain of imprisonment.[62] Agricultural workers who
left service were to be imprisoned, as well as those who hired them.
Employers who transgressed were to pay double to those aggrieved.
Lords of towns or manors were to be "pursued" for triple the amount
they offered. Artificers were to accept only their customary prices,
and victuallers were to charge moderately. No one was to give anything to an able beggar. In the subsequent statute it was stipulated
that agricultural workers were to be hired by the year, and wages
for various services were specified. Such workmen wishing to be
hired were to bring their implements to town and be hired pub-
licly where everyone could see and hear. Wages of various trades
were specified and prison terms set for offenders. To make these
provisions more attractive it was stipulated that amercements were
to be used in relief of the fifteenths and the tenths, the surplus,
if any, being turned over to the nearest poor town. Measurements
of cloths were specified and lax ulnagers were to be punished. There
were regulations concerning victuals, a clause against forestalling
(a common practice in towns, expecially among women), and one
against the installation of mills, weirs, or kiddles in rivers where
they might impede traffic. Sheriffs were forbidden, once more, to
take fees from those entering or leaving prison, and justices were
required to sit four times a year. The statute was supplemented
in 1360–1361 (34 Ed III 9),[63] specifying terms of imprisonment
and stipulating that carpenters and masons were to work by the
day rather than by the week. Fugitive laborers were to be outlawed
and might be branded on the forehead with an *F* for falsity. Mayors and bailiffs of towns who refused to deliver fugitives might be
fined £10. As we have seen, there was a complaint in Parliament
in 1378 that agricultural laborers fled to towns so that husbandry

was difficult. Efforts to enforce these statutes, especially after 1368 when the justices of the peace were given jurisdiction, were often assiduous, and these labors may have done much to stimulate the revolt of 1381.[64] However, the problem being addressed was by no means solved, as the petitions and statutes of Richard's reign reveal.

There was, for example, a series of complaints about improperly measured cloths, to one of which I shall return in a moment.[65] Although the great revolt itself was brought under control, it evidently stimulated a great deal of criminal activity, and a statute was passed in 1383 (7 R II 6)[66] against robbery, theft, and manslaughter by men riding in routs. Two years later another was issued against villeins who fled to cities and there brought suit against their lords for freedom (9 R II 2).[67] There was an outbreak of pestilence in 1383 that may have intensified the demand for higher agricultural wages, for it was decreed in 1388 (12 R II 3)[68] that servants and apprentices of artificers might be conscripted to help at harvest time. This was followed by a series of new labor statutes (12 R II 4–7)[69] concerning manorial servants. The preamble is instructive: "Because that servants and laborers will not, nor by a long season would, serve and labor without outrageous and excessive hire, and much more than hath been given to such laborers and servants in any time past, so that for scarcity of the said laborers and servants, the husbands and landtenants may not pay their rents, nor scarcely live upon their lands ... it is accorded and assented that the bailiff for husbandry shall take by the year 13s 4d, and his clothing once a year at the most." The master hine was to have 10s, the shepherd 10s, the oxherd 6s 8d, the swineherd 6s, a woman laborer 6s, a deye 6s, a driver of the plow 7s at the most, and every other laborer or servant according to his degree. Similar stipulations were made concerning servants of artisans in towns. As Nora Ritchie has shown, workers were often demanding double or treble the amounts stipulated.[70] It was further decreed (c.5) that those who labor at husbandry under the age of twelve should "abide at the same labor, without being put to any mystery or handicraft." Moreover (c. 60), that "no servant of husbandry, or laborer, nor servant of artificer, nor of victualler, shall from henceforth bear any buckler, sword, nor dagger" except in the company of their masters or when going on message for them. They should instead have bows and arrows and "leave all playing at tennis or football, and other games called coits, dice, or casting the stone, or kailes [skittles] and other such importune games."[71] No servant was to leave his hundred, rape, or wapentake at the end of his term, except in some areas where it was customary, and none was to go on pilgrimage without a letter patent indicating the dates of departure and return. The justices of the peace (c. 10)[72] were ordered to inquire whether "mayors, bailiffs, stewards, constables, and jailers have done execution of the said ordinance," and offenders were to be fined 100s. Moreover, the justices were now to receive their wages from the sheriff, no steward was to be assigned to commissions of the peace (a provision almost immediately repealed[73]), and no association was to be made after the first appointment. The provision regarding town officials was evidently ineffective, for in 1391 the commons complained (15 R II 11)[74] that many villeins who fled to franchised towns could neither be approached nor apprehended, much less judged by their lords. Town governments were generally sensitive about their jurisdictions.[75] Complaints about liveries were expanded in 1388, for the commons wished to abolish not only liveries of temporal and spiritual lords, but also liveries of guilds and fraternities, which evidently gave them the appearance of being covins, or conspiracies.[76] In 1389–1390 the justices of the peace were cautioned to use discretion concerning wages because of fluctuations in the price of grain (13 R II 1.8).[77] And a statute was issued against inferior west-country cloths (13 R II 1.11),[78] which were tacked and folded for sale, concealing the fact that the cloth inside might be bruised, unevenly dyed, of inconsistent width, or made from various grades of wool. When merchants sold these cloths abroad they were "many times in danger to be slain, and sometimes imprisoned, and put to fine and ransom." This may lead us to wonder about the Wife of Bath, who was a west-country clothier.

The general situation revealed in the parliamentary records is confirmed when we consult manorial or town records. For example, the court records for John of Gaunt's Ingoldmells manor reveal eleven instances of tenants leaving the manor for excessive wages elsewhere between 1386 and 1389.[79] In an effort to maintain their incomes many manorial lords leased their demesnes, often to a single tenant, who could afford to pay the higher wages being demanded, and there was a widespread tendency to commute labor services for rents. Especially after the pestilence of 1360 many traditional peasant families disappeared, and their holdings, often consolidated into larger units, were taken over by rent-paying tenants without family ties to the land and interested chiefly in profits. Naturally, they were often employers of hired labor. At the same time workers in towns were demanding and receiving higher pay, and merchants and tradesmen were not only asking higher prices but selling defective goods, ranging from putrid meat or old fish to poorly tanned leather, candles without wicks, or the defective cloths just mentioned.[80] It is significant, I believe, that the word commonly used for excessive wages or prices was *extortion*. That is, workers and merchants from the point of view of contemporaries were doing exactly the same kind of thing that corrupt archdeacons, summoners, sheriffs, bailiffs, coroners, lawyers, or royal purveyors were doing. They were, at the same time, showing little interest in "the common profit" either of their own manors, towns, or shires, or of the realm as a whole. It must have seemed that the old ideals of fidelity and truth were rapidly vanishing from the face of the earth.

III.

Indeed, this is the theme of Chaucer's "Lak of Stedfastnesse," a balade addressed to King Richard, perhaps on his assumption of power in May, 1389.[81] It begins with a complaint that although a man's word was once an obligation, word and deed now bear little resemblance, for the world is now turned upside-down for meed and willfulness. A man is considered able if he can wrong or oppress his neighbor; covetousness has blinded discretion and "all is lost for lack of steadfastness." Chaucer urges the king to "hate extortion," to show his sword of castigation, to fear God, do law, love truth and worthiness, and to wed his people to steadfastness. Under the circumstances this was a large order. But the ideals are traditional, reflecting the kind of moral doctrines that Chaucer might well have found in John of Salisbury. The later fourteenth century was in many ways out of tune with them. It has been called an "age of ambition"[82] characterized by a widespread desire for self-aggrandizement and by a spirit of enterprise. The enterprise was not by any means always illegal, but even when it was not it seemed inconsistent with long-cherished ideals. A very brief glance at the General Prologue to the *Canterbury Tales* will show, I believe, that Chaucer used that work as a humorously exaggerated attack on the lack of "steadfastness" in the hierarchy of the realm. However, I think that we should consider the characters not as being "realistic," or even as "personalities," but instead as presentations of the ideals or the weaknesses of the groups presented.

Leaving aside for a moment the "idealized" characters, including the Knight with his modest entourage and his less worthy son, we encounter first the Prioress of the fashionable Benedictine nunnery of St. Leonard at Stratford at Bow.[83] Her studied but actually rather inept courtly manners, in part derived from the worldly advice of the Old Whore in the *Roman de la rose*, her false sentimental sensitivity that offers a poor substitute for true charity, her extravagant care for her little dogs, and her very expensive rosary with its dubious motto combine to form a picture of worldliness entirely inconsistent with traditional notions of what a nun should be.[84] Steadfastness is even less evident in the Monk, who holds not only his rule but monastic ideals generally in contempt, caring nothing for either work or study. In other words, he is from a monastic point of view "lawless." He loves "venery," probably of both kinds, is an "outrider" or bailiff errant, whose "dainty" horses are ostentatiously caparisoned as he is himself with expensively furred sleeves. He is well-fed, a lover of roast swan, the most expensive poultry available. Clearly, his wealth is not consistent with the usual monastic ideals. The Friar has no interest whatsoever in spiritual penances, but only in money, which he accepts as a substitute for true repentance. He is himself lecherous, a great singer who frequents tavers where he is familiar with barmaids. He likes especially the company of franklins, or wealthy landholders not of noble rank, of wealthy victuallers, or of any persons who can furnish him profit. In fact, he can even get a farthing from a poor widow. At "love-days" offering opportunities for maintenance he dresses like a master or a pope. The contemplative orders are obviously subject to the same kinds of weaknesses we have seen among other groups.

Chaucer turns next to the Merchant, a dealer in wool,[85] who although in debt always talks about his profits. He makes money in the exchange in violation of a statute of 1351 (25 Ed III 5.12)[86] and practices illegal usury, or what Chaucer calls "chevysaunce," against which there was a parliamentary petition in 1390.[87] The

Sergeant of the Law, who often served as a justice in assize, had
many "fees and robes," which means that he was a "maintainer,"
and was a great purchaser of land in fee simple, probably through
champerty. He knew all the cases and judgments since the time
of King William, or before the time of legal memory,[88] an impossible achievement the implication of which is that he could readily
cite fictitious precedents for his own purposes. With him was his
friend the Franklin, who had been a sheriff and justice of the peace,
offices he found to be extremely profitable and through which he
became a wealthy vavasour or subtenant so that he could serve day-
long feasts of costly fowl and fish with fine wines and rare sauces
to the great men of the shire during sessions. Chaucer has these
legal gentlemen, both of whom attended Parliament, ride along
together, clearly suggesting cooperation in maintenance.

The so-called "guildsmen," actually members of a parish frater-
nity, ostentatiously dressed in liveries with expensive knives (illegal in the City of London), girdles, and pouches, seem to their
wives (who would like to be treated like ladies) worthy to become
aldermen. For they have gained through their "wisdom" sufficient
property and income. But no carpenter, weaver, dyer, or tapicer
became a London alderman. These are small artificers who have
clearly profited from high prices. To keep their appetites satisfied
they have brought with them their own cook, who, appropriately,
prepares dubious white sauce.

There is also a Shipman who steals wine from sleeping merchants
on his return from Bordeaux, makes his enemies walk the plank,
and knows all the creeks in Brittany and Spain, where he can readily engage in smuggling. A Physician was there who could impress
his patients with references to famous authorities much in the same
way that the Sergeant of Law could cite cases and judgments. He
connives with his friend the apothecary to their mutual profit. He
is generally penurious, but extravagant in his dress to make a good
impression. Pestilences are especially profitable to him, and he is
very fond of gold.

One of the most striking of Chaucer's figures is the Wife of Bath
who probably owes her prominence to the fact that the cloth industry was flourishing in rural areas away from the control of the
guilds and attracting many agricultural workers. She has become
such a prominent member of her community that she proudly insists on being first at the offering in church, where she is expen-

sively decked out in coverchiefs. Her hose are of the most expensive woolens, scarlet in grain (closely sheared wool dyed in kermes). She has been profitably married to five husbands, has accumulated enough wealth to make expensive pilgrimages, although she "wanders from the way" a great deal, and is expert in the "old dance" of love. We can be justly suspicious of the quality of her west-country cloths.[89] But the pilgrims are led out of town by a drunken Miller playing a bagpipe, a foul-mouthed character who practices both theft and extortion, especially oppressive to the poor who depend on his services for the preparation of their bread and gruel. The rear of the procession is occupied by the Reeve, a kind of competitor in extortion among the rural workers. He has risen to his office from his position as a manorial carpenter. His accounts are never in arrears, but he keeps his superior, the bailiff, and his fellow-servants on the manor in fear of him through his knowledge of their little conspiracies, which he fails to report as he should to the manorial court. Meanwhile, he steals from his lord but subtly pleases him by giving or lending him his own goods.[90] He carries a rusty blade at his side in violation of the Statute of 1388. There is a Manciple of a temple who can profit greatly from his purchases of victuals in spite of the legal astuteness of his masters. The last two pilgrims, except for the host, are again ecclesiastics: a corrupt Summoner who would allow a man to have his concubine for a quart of wine, and an extortionate Pardoner, who with false relics earned more money in a day than the local parson gained in two months. And the Host himself, a worthy burgess, and exactly the kind of man the Friar likes to keep company with, turns out in the course of the journey to be amusingly deaf to the implications of the tales he hears.

It is not surprising, actually, that the majority of the characters on the road to Canterbury are singularly lacking in what Chaucer called "steadfastness." They not only deviate from the standards of behavior accepted as norms for their groups, but are frequently lawless, either explicitly or by implication. They illustrate very well the kinds of things concerning which the men of the shire courts, boroughs, and clerical convocations were deeply troubled, and which they hoped those they sent to Parliament would seek to remedy. Since Chaucer was a courtier, associated with the chamber, whose duties brought him into close contact with the exchequer and the courts, and whose friends at court were lords of manors, while some

of his acquaintances were members of Parliament or sheriffs like
Sir Arnold Savage, or bishops and other ecclesiastics, this fact is
hardly surprising. The ideal characters in his General Prologue,
who are steadfast in their offices, are reminders of goals to be de-
sired. The lack of success of English chivalry either in maintain-
ing England's traditional holdings and allies abroad or in protecting the realm from foreign incursions, which became an acute problem in 1386, was often attributed to the lack of virtue among chivalric leaders, especially with regard to sexual conduct.[91] Chaucer's
Knight, however, is worthy, wise, and humble; he loves chivalry,
truth, honor, generosity, and courtesy, and has fought gloriously
against the heathen. His son the Squire has been fighting Christians in areas reminiscent of Bishop Despencer's disgraceful crusade, not "in his lord's war," but in hopes to stand in the grace of
his lady. The contrast between the humble Knight and the fash-
ionably dressed Squire with his devotion to the seductive arts,
reminiscent of John of Salisbury's Terentian braggart soldiers, is
an obvious comment on chivalric decay. The Knight, unlike many
of his degree who rode with ostentatious retinues,[92] is attended
only by his son and one servant, his forester, who rides armed in
the company of his lord but carries the bow and arrows appropriate to his station. The Clerk, who holds neither ecclesiastic nor
secular office, studies hard and prays for those who have supported
him at school. He speaks without verbosity of moral virtue. The
Parson works tirelessly in his parish, which he does not desert for
an easy position in London. He is content with a meager sufficiency,
refrains from excommunicating the poor who cannot pay their
tithes, and generally sets a good example in his own conduct for
the ideals and virtues he preaches. Finally, his brother the Plowman follows the precepts of charity, works willingly to help his poor
neighbors without pay, and faithfully pays his tithes.

As I indicated at the outset it would be difficult to ascribe the
social changes that disturbed Chaucer to the effects of pestilence
alone. His first long poem, *The Book of the Duchess*, celebrates the
virtues of Blanche of Lancaster, who died of pestilence. He undoubtedly knew that the change in King Edward came after his
queen died of pestilence. Pestilence plays a large part in only one
of the Canterbury Tales, the *Pardoner's Tale*, and there it leads to
an irrational abandonment of brotherly obligations in a deadly quest
for gold. Chaucer was undoubtedly aware that its effect on the realm

as a whole, which had long been susceptible to this weakness, might be very similar.

In conclusion, I should like to say that modern cynicism and sentimentality, reinforced by romantic or post-romantic political sensibilities, have often led to a denigration of Chaucer's ideal characters and to an elevation of his rogues. But the picture of Chaucer that results would have made him a mere trifler in his own time, unworthy of the respect as a "philosopher" he achieved among his contemporaries and the more discerning of his admirers in the fifteenth and sixteenth centuries. I do not think we shall understand him very well unless we can become better acquainted with the issues and attitudes of his own time, as well as with the intellectual and literary traditions he inherited.

Notes

1. *Statutes of the Realm* (London, 1810–1828), 1. 396–97, (hereafter *SR*). May McKisack, *The Fourteenth Century* (Oxford, 1959), p. 396, calls the pardon a "colossal bribe," but this may be a little extreme. Edward's concern for his people, which he frequently expressed, should not be regarded simply as a device for gaining revenue.

2. On Edward's reaction to pestilence, see J. F. D. Shrewsbury, *A History of Bubonic Plague in Medieval England* (Oxford, 1975), p. 68. Cf. on war John Barnie, *War in Medieval English Society* (Ithaca, 1974), p. 28. And generally, see the "Verses on the Earthquake of 1382," in Carleton Brown, ed., *Religious Lyrics of the Fourteenth Century* (Oxford, 1924), no. 113, pp. 186–88.

3. *SR*, 1. 364–65. Returned military leaders with distinguished careers were also difficult to control. For example, Sir Matthew Gurney fought in France and Spain after 1340, and with the companies after the treaty of Bretigny. He was at Auray in 1364. In 1388, at age eighty, he acted as constable for Edmund of York, who went to Spain to aid Gaunt. He and his lawyer, John Janet, engaged in very dubious activities at home. Sir Matthew was indicted for trespass in 1380, but obtained a writ *supersedeas*. In 1381 he was pardoned for contempts, trespasses, and extortions. In 1385 he was in trouble for mayhem, but obtained another *supersedeas*. Nevertheless, he served as JP in 1381–1385, as well as being named in commissions of oyer and terminer, and, in addition, was constable for the court of chivalry. He was sued by a London weaver in 1388, who alleged that he and John Janet had imprisoned him un-

til he promised to pay Sir Matthew, who alleged that he was his serf, £1000 for manumission. Sir Matthew was named on peace commissions in 1388–1392 and became a member of the royal council under Henry IV. He died finally at the age of 97. See Isobel D. Thornley and T. F. T. Plucknett, *Year Books of Richard II: 11 R II* (Ames Foundation, 1937), pp. xiii–xvi and 170–74. Another example is afforded by Richard de Aske of Aughton, who, although he received various pardons for felonies because of his service in France, frequently served on commissions, including oyer and terminer and sewers. See Bertha Haven Putnam, *Yorkshire Sessions of the Peace*, Yorkshire Archaeological Society, Record Series, vol. 100 (1939), pp. xxxix–xl.

4. For the effects on Southampton, for example, see Colin Platt, *Medieval Southampton* (London and Boston, 1973), pp. 125–28.

5. Cf. George Holmes, *The Good Parliament* (Oxford, 1975), p. 90.

6. See J. Moisant, ed., *Speculo regis Edwardi III* (Recensio A) (Paris, 1891), p. 96.

7. The events surrounding this action are described in detail by G. L. Harriss, *King, Parliament, and Public Finance to 1369* (Oxford, 1975), chapters twelve and thirteen.

8. 4 Ed III 3, 4, *SR*, 1. 262; 5 Ed III 2, p. 266; 10 Ed III 2.1, p. 276; 14 Ed III 1.19, p. 288; 18 Ed III 2.7, p. 301; 25 Ed III 5.1, p. 319; 28 Ed III 12, p. 347; 34 Ed III 2,3, p. 365; 36 Ed III 1.2,3,4, p. 371.

9. *SR*, 1. 283.

10. Traditionally the manorial bailiff of a monastery was a cellarer. At St. Peter, Westminster, there were two cellarers, one "external" who oversaw the manors, and the other "internal." When the external cellarer spent several days in the monastery he took over the duties of the internal cellarer, who remained in the cloister. See Edward Maunde Thompson, ed., *Customary of the Benedictine Monasteries of Saint Augustine, Canterbury and Saint Peter, Westminster*, 2 vols., Henry Bradshaw Society vol. 28 (1904), 2:69. At St. Albans Abbey the cellarer acted as a kind of itinerant justice at the biennial Halimotes. See A. E. Levett, "The Court and Court Rolls of St. Albans Abbey," *TRHS*, 4th ser. 8 (1924): 60. The Benedictine Rule specifies that the cellarer should be "wise, mature in conduct, temperate, not an excessive eater, not proud, excitable, offensive, dilatory, or wasteful, but God-fearing, and like a father to the whole community." He should, moreover, be above all humble. See *The Rule of St. Benedict in Latin and English with Notes,* ed. Timothy Fry, O.S.B. (Collegeville, Minn., 1981), pp. 227, 229. Chaucer's monk hardly rides resplendent in these virtues.

11. *SR*, 1. 346. This statute was not consistently enforced.

12. Ibid., 1. 389.

13. Ibid., 1. 394.

14. On the duties of escheators, see *SR*, 1. 238–41.

15. Ibid., 1. 367–68.

16. Ibid., 1. 303–6. The oath covering the points of the Ordinance is given at length.

17. I cite only New Testament examples: Acts 10:34; Rom. 2:11; Eph. 6:9; James 2:9; 1 Pet. 1:17; Jude 16.

18. Cf. Ps. 14:5, a verse that plays an important part in *Piers Plowman*. See D. W. Robertson, Jr., and B. F. Huppé, *Piers Plowman and Scriptural Tradition* (Princeton, 1951), pp. 53–57, 60, 161, 210.

19. *SR*, 2. 37. For a discussion of parliamentary efforts to stem judicial corruption after the Revolt, see J. R. Madicott, *Law and Lordship: Royal Justices as Retainers in Thirteenth and Fourteenth Century England*, Past and Present Society, Supplement 4 (1978), pp. 64ff.

20. *SR*, 1. 360. For a definition, see *SR*, 1. 145.

21. Ibid., 1. 366.

22. Ibid., 1. 364–65. These justices replaced the Keepers of the Peace.

23. 2 Ed III 2, *SR*, 1. 257–58; 10 Ed III 1.3, p. 275; 14 Ed III 1.15, p. 286; 27 Ed III 1.2, p. 330. However, felonies continued to be pardoned for a fee.

24. R. F. Hunnisett, *Bedfordshire Coroner's Rolls*, Bedfordshire Historical Record Society, vol. 41 (1961), p. vi, observes, "All coroners practiced moderate extortion; bribes became an invariable prelude to the performance of their duties, and some coroners were much more oppressive." For an instance of a coroner who extorted 6s 8d from a man for viewing a corpse, see Bertha Haven Putnam, *Proceedings of the Justices of the Peace in the Fourteenth and Fifteenth Centuries* (Ames Foundation, 1938), p. 446. A Yorkshire coroner was fined for stealing 6s 8d from a corpse. See Putnam, *Yorkshire Sessions*, p. 108.

25. E.g., see the last will of William Donne, archdeacon of Leicester, as cited by A. H. Thompson, *The English Clergy and Their Organization in Later Middle Ages* (Oxford, 1947), pp. 60–61, who asked God's forgiveness for exactions and extortions, in which, he said, he merely followed the example of his brethren. On the specific activities of archdeacons, see Jean Scammell, "The Rural Chapter in England from the Eleventh to the Fourteenth Century," *EHR* 86 (1971): 1–21. The fact (pp. 17–18) that both the innocent and the guilty would pay to avoid citation partly explains the opportunity for extortion. Archdeacons sometimes also extorted money for wills. See Margaret Aston, *Thomas Arundel* (Oxford, 1967), pp. 93–94. The following pages contain evidence of extortion by archdeacons' officials. Summoners or apparitors were notorious. See Brian L. Woodcock, *Medieval Ecclesiastical Courts in the Diocese of Canterbury* (Oxford, 1952), pp. 49, 111. Rural Deans, with whom archdeacons were associated, were also tempted in the same way. For a specific example, see Elizabeth Gurnsey Kimball, *Rolls of the Gloucestershire Sessions of the Peace, 1361–1398*, Transactions of the Bristol and Gloucestershire Archaeological Society, vol. 62 (1942), p. 128.

26. The term "feudal system" was first used in England in the seventeenth century. *Feudalism* is an artificial construct originating in the minds of historians, who have "defined" it in various ways and who frequently employ it very loosely. Its "origins," "history," and "decline" depend entirely on the definition being used. That is, it can be said to have "ended" in the later thirteenth century, in the Renaissance, at the time of the French Revolution, or, in England, with the passage of the Agricultural Holding Act of 1923. Similarly, its "origins" can be located in different times and places. Like many other "isms" it is a convenient label that often carries emotional overtones,

although its concrete referents are vague. European societies called "feudal"
were always complex with wide local variations and were always undergoing
fairly rapid changes, a fact that the term tends to obscure.

27. *SR*, 1. 106. A. W. B. Simpson, *An Introduction to the History of the Land
Law* (Oxford, 1961), p. 51, calls the statute "a striking illustration of the lack
of importance which by this time was attached to the personal relationship
of lord and tenant; lords were more interested in protecting their incidents
than in selecting their tenants." The statute effectively discouraged grants in
fee farm. But it did not prevent the granting of lucrative sinecures to faithful
retainers.

28. We may compare the career of Lord John Fitzwalter of Essex with that
of Sir Matthew Gurney (above, n. 3). For Lord John Fitzwalter, see Elizabeth
Chapin Furber, *Essex Sessions of the Peace 1351, 1377–79*, Essex Archaeological
Society Occasional Publications, vol. 3 (1953), pp. 61–62. Lord John's lands
were seized by the king, whereas Sir Matthew, who had a good lawyer, continued in royal favor.

29. *SR*, 2. 2–3. Cf. *Rotuli parliamentorum* (Record Commission, 1783) 3. 21
(hereafter *RP*). For an example of such a person from Wiltshire, see Putnam,
Proceedings before the Justices of the Peace, pp. 385–86.

30. Cf. R. B. Dobson, *The Peasants' Revolt of 1381* (London, 1970), pp.
13–15; M. M. Postan, *The Medieval Economy and Society* (Berkeley and Los
Angeles, 1972), pp. 153–54. The latter points out that the facts do not fit the
theory that the revolt was "a typical instance of the working class revolt against
repression." I might add that the latter view is a typical example of the tendency among historians to view the past in the light of current "isms" and their
attendant prejudices.

31. An effort to revive this legislation, which had been neglected, failed in
1384, *RP*, 3. 201.

32. Ibid., 3. 21.

33. Ibid., 3. 19–20. This complaint was repeated in the following year and
brought a temporary remedy.

34. *SR*. 2. 114. But this statute did not prevent extortion among sheriffs.

35. Dorothy Bruce Weske, *Convocation of Clergy* (London, 1937), pp. 72–72.
Cf. *RP*, 3. 26, where escheators are also mentioned. Cf. "The Song Against
Sheriffs" quoted by Helen M. Cam, *The Hundred and the Hundred Rolls* (London, 1930), p. 106. For an example of lay interference with an ecclesiastical
court, see Elizabeth Gurnsey Kimball, *Some Sessions of the Peace in Lincolnshire*,
2 vols., Lincoln Record Society, vol. 56 (1962), 2:8. In this instance, the
perpetrator, one John Racy, was later (p. 179) indicted for being a common
thief who had stolen a horse.

36. *RP*, 3. 25; cf. *SR*, 1. 43. See n. 25, above. In 1392 John Lawrence,
registrar of the bishop of Winchester, was indicted in Hampshire for having
taken 13s 4d "by extortion" for probate of a will, 40s from another for the same
service, and 10s and a silver seal worth 10s from two other executors. See
G. O. Sayles, *Select Cases in the Court of King's Bench*, Selden Society, vol. 7
(1971), pp. 82–83. Even a bishop might be extortionate. Thus Henry of Wake-
field, bishop of Worcester, and his suffragan were indicted for extorting money

for consecrating chapels and altars. See Elizabeth Gurnsey Kimball, *Some War-wickshire and Coventry Sessions of the Peace, 1377–1397*, Dugdale Society, vol. 16 (1939), pp. 105–6.

37. *RP*, 3. 43. Cf. n. 25, above.

38. Ibid., 3. 46.

39. Cf. on the effects of the cutlery trade at Thaxted, Nora Ritchie, "Labour Conditions in Essex in the Reign of Richard II," in *Essays in Economic History*, ed. E. M. Carus-Wilson, vol. 2 (London, 1962), p. 93. On the manor of Thaxted the working of demesne lands by tenants except for a few acres of mowing ended in 1362, and the elaborate peasant hierarchy became a legal fiction. See K. C. Newton, *Thaxted*, Essex Record Office Publications, vol. 33 (Chelmsford, 1960), pp. 25–26, and on the cutlery trade there, pp. 20–23. The cloth trade was especially attractive to agricultural workers in some areas. See A. R. Bridbury, *England and the Salt Trade in the Later Middle Ages* (Oxford, 1955), pp. 36–37. Although the general effect of the cloth industry has been denied, it clearly did offer opportunities for agricultural workers where it flourished, as did other trades elsewhere.

40. *SR*, 2. 9.

41. Ibid.

42. *RP*, 3. 64.

43. Ibid., 3. 80.

44. Ibid., 3. 80–81.

45. Ibid., 3. 81.

46. Ibid., repeated in the following year, *RP*, 3. 94.

47. *SR*, 2. 14.

48. *RP*, 3. 83–85.

49. Ibid., 3. 94.

50. Sir Goronwy Edwards, *The Second Century of the English Parliament* (Oxford, 1979), pp. 17–31.

51. E. Powell, *The Rising in East Anglia* (Cambridge, 1896), p. 4.

52. *RP*, 3. 100–101.

53. Ibid., 3. 140. We can understand why the devil in the *Friar's Tale* should appear as a bailiff.

54. Ibid., 3. 201, 280, 308.

55. Ibid., 3. 138; *SR*, 2. 35.

56. Barbara Hanawalt, *Crime in East Anglia in the Fourteenth Century: Norfolk Gaol Delivery Rolls, 1302–16*, Norfolk Record Society, vol. 44 (1976), pp. 14–15.

57. On high prices in 1361–1365 see A. R. Bridbury, "The Black Death," *EcHR*, 2nd ser. 26 (1973): 584.

58. John Bellamy, *Crime and Public Order in the Later Middle Ages* (London and Toronto, 1973), p. 6. For a local example, see J. A. Raftis, *Warboys* (Toronto, 1974), pp. 220–21.

59. L. F. Salzman, *English Trade in the Middle Ages* (Oxford, 1931), p. 284.

60. *SR*, 1. 307–8.

61. Ibid., 1. 311–16.

62. For a case involving this provision, see Sayles, *Select Cases*, vol. 7, pp. 60–61.

63. *SR*, 1. 366.
64. Cf. Bridbury, "The Black Death," p. 585.
65. E.g., *RP*, 3. 159.
66. *SR*, 2. 33; cf. c. 15, p. 35.
67. Ibid., 2. 38.
68. Ibid., 2. 56.
69. Ibid., 2. 57–58.
70. Ritchie, "Labour Conditions in Essex," pp. 91–111; cf. McKisack, *The Fourteenth Century*, pp. 339–40.
71. "Importune" or troublesome games had already come to the attention of local courts. For example, in 1373 six men at Colchester were accused of being common dice players, and one for being "a common player of chess." All were said to stay awake at night and to frequent taverns. And in 1375 three men were fined 6d each for playing unlawful games, and agreed to pay 6s 8d each if they were caught again. See I. H. Jeayes, *Court Rolls of the Borough of Colchester*, vol. 3 (Colchester, 1941), pp. 17, 81. The tenants of the Durham vill of Hetheworths were forbidden to play at dice on pain of 20s. Football ("soccer"), which led (as it apparently still does) to "gravis contencio et contumelia" was forbidden in 1381. See W. H. Longstreet and John Booth, *Halmota Prioratus Dunelmensis*, Surtees Society, vol. 82 (1889), pp. 166, 171. At Castle Combe such games were still being punished in the Renaissance. See J. Poulet Scrope, *Castle Combe* (London, 1852), pp. 330, 332, 335. The dice playing of Chaucer's Franklin's young son is reprehensible aside from the fact that it involves loss of money, which seems to disturb the Franklin. Ironically, many noblemen were fond of it.
72. *SR*, 2. 58–59.
73. Ibid., 2. 62–63.
74. *RP*, 3. 296.
75. This fact is amusingly illustrated by the treatment of approvers (or convicted felons who obtained temporary respite by identifying and offering to prove themselves upon unidentified accomplices) who came from outside the liberty of Fordwick, the old port of Canterbury. Such an approver should enter the liberty with his equipment (probably a battle-ax with a leather blade and a leather jerkin). The custom of the borough as recorded by Mary Bateson, *Borough Customs*, Selden Society, vol. 1 (1904), p. 33, ran as follows. "He shall be led to the running water called the Stour, and he shall stand in that water up to his navel, with his equipment, in the manner of an approver, ready, as aforesaid, to prove his appeal. And the said freeman thus appealed shall come in a rowboat of three benches in the same river opposite the said approver, and the freeman shall wear a garment called a *skerp* (leather jacket), and shall have a weapon called an oar three yards in length, and his boat shall be made fast by a rope to the quay, and in the said water he shall fight with the said approver until the duel between them is finished." One can imagine the joy of the citizens if and when this custom was implemented.
76. *RP*, 3. 266.
77. *SR*, 2. 63. Cf. *RP*, 3. 272.
78. *SR*, 2. 64.

79. W. O. Massingberd, *Court Rolls of the Manor of Ingoldmells* (London, 1902), pp. 180-81, 185, 186.

80. W. H. Stevenson, *Records of the Borough of Nottingham*, vol. 1 (London, 1882), pp. 269-73, 315, 317-19. Cf. Ritchie, "Labour Conditions," pp. 95-96.

81. Geoffrey Chaucer, *The Works of Geoffrey Chaucer*, ed. F. N. Robinson, 2nd ed. (Cambridge, Mass., 1957), p. 537.

82. See especially F. R. H. Du Boulay, *An Age of Ambition: English Society in the Late Middle Ages* (London, 1970). May McKisack, *The Parliamentary Representation of the English Boroughs During the Late Middle Ages* (Oxford, 1932), p. 43, said that "in spite of the Black Death" and "the drain of the French war" the later fourteenth century was a time of "increasing municipal prosperity." More recent studies are more likely to emphasize prosperity in both agriculture and trade as a *result* of the Black Death, which is said to have reduced overpopulation. See most recently John Hatcher, *Plague, Population and the English Economy* (Economic History Society, 1977), pp. 31-34, who calls attention to the fact (p. 34) that the prosperity of the lesser folk outraged moralists like the chronicler Knighton, who in 1388 wrote of "the elation of the inferior people in dress and accoutrements ... so that one person cannot be distinguished from another either in splendor of dress or belongings, neither poor from rich nor servant from master."

83. On the nunnery, see H. P. F. King, "The Priory of Stratford at Bow," *Victoria County History: Middlesex* 1 (1969): 151-59. In 1380-1381 there were only fourteen nuns, one of whom was called "Argentyn."

84. See most recently Chauncey Wood, "Chaucer's Portrait of the Prioress," in *Signs and Symbols in Chaucer's Poetry*, ed. John P. Hermann and John J. Burke, Jr. (University, Alabama, 1981), pp. 81-100.

85. The Merchant is concerned about the safety of shipping "Bitwixe Middleburghe and Orwelle." After the French advance in Flanders in 1383 wool was sent to Middleburg, which became a compulsory staple in 1384. But in January 1387 convoys had to be employed between the two ports. The staple was restored to Calais in 1389. See T. H. Lloyd, *The English Wool Trade in the Middle Ages* (Cambridge, 1977), pp. 230-31. The Merchant's concern thus identifies his trade for Chaucer's audience and at the same time affords us an approximate date for the composition of the Prologue, or at least for this part of it.

86. *SR*, 1. 322.

87. *RP*, 3. 280-81. The commons petitioned that since both lay and spiritual lords practice "the abhominable vice of usury" and call it "chevance" the old statutes concerning usury should be confirmed. *Chevance* is clearly a variant of the term Chaucer uses.

88. On the limit of legal memory, see C. R. Cheney, *Handbook of Dates for Students of English History* (London, 1961), p. 65.

89. Cf. my article " 'And for My Land Thus Hastow Mordred Me?': Land Tenure, the Cloth Industry, and the Wife of Bath," *ChaucR* 14 (1980): 403-20.

90. For an example of a tyrannical reeve, see P. D. A. Harvey, *Manorial Records of Cuxham*, Oxfordshire Record Society, vol. 50 (1976), p. 669. Here the whole homage was in mercy for concealing the transgressions of the reeve

for four years (clearly through fear). He had let his animals into the lord's pasture, stolen a small ash tree, and abetted a miller who stole grain from the lord's granary. For some light on Chaucer's lines

> Wel koude he kepe a gerner and a bynne;
> Ther was noon auditour koude on him wynne,

see Eleanor Searle, *Lordship and Community: Battle Abbey and its Banlieu* (Toronto, 1974), pp. 316–18.

91. I have discussed this point at length in an article now in preparation, "The Probable Date and Purpose of Chaucer's *Troilus*."

92. See K. B. McFarlane, *The Nobility of Later Medieval England* (Oxford, 1973), pp. 105–12.

'he hath a thousand slayn this pestilence':
the Iconography of the plague
in the Late middle ages

John B. Friedman

PERHAPS THE MOST STRIKING FEATURE of medieval art dealing with the plague is its indirection. That is, in an age
when an estimated one-third of Europe's population died
of disease, surprisingly few manuscript miniatures and wall paintings depict the sick and dying. The scarcity of contemporary plague
imagery is reflected in modern studies[1] of the Black Death of 1348
and its aftermath, which have relied heavily upon Renaissance art
for illustration. For example, Jean-Noël Biraben's recent two-volume
Les hommes et la peste has a 227-page bibliography, and some 200
pages of graphs, charts, and tables dealing with all manner of
medical, demographic, and economic issues. And yet, of its twenty illustrations, only four are medieval, and of these, only two are
from manuscript painting.[2]

Those scholars who have concerned themselves specifically with
the plague's impact on medieval art have concentrated on two
motifs—the Dance of Death[3] and the Three Living and Three
Dead[4]—as well as on the development of the transi tomb.[5] Unfortunately, the first two motifs have only an implied association
with the disease,[6] since their themes are mortality in general and
not the cause of death, while funerary art never depicts plague victims during their illness.[7]

The relatively small amount of what we might term direct "re-
portage" imagery is not, however, evidence of unconcern for the
subject. Rather, it reflects the very slow development of an artistic
vocabulary by which to describe the plague, in a period when
painters preferred to copy or adapt earlier pictures. More important, painting and sculpture of the sick and dying comprises only
a part of the broad range of medieval responses to the epidemic,
in art as in literature. Such responses also include the explanations

put forth for the disease and — depending on which explanation one favored — the means proposed for avoiding it. Treatments of these subjects in medieval art were, unlike the Dance of Death and other such motifs belonging to the *memento mori* tradition, direct and explicit statements about the plague. They contributed significantly to the imagery that gradually came to be associated with the disease, yet their contribution has gone largely unexamined.

The art of the late Middle Ages reveals two widely held views of the plague's origin and the ways in which fourteenth- and fifteenth-century Europeans hoped to protect themselves from it. The first view, associated with medicine, was that the plague was caused by a malign conjunction of planets or by the "drying" action of comets, which produced droughts, locusts, and foul air that swept across Europe from the east. The second view, associated with the Church, was that the plague was God's punishment for man's sins, against which penance and the help of an intercessor, such as Saint Sebastian, were the only remedies.[8] For example, a Scots annalist describing the plague's universal devastation, commented "cujus summa salus est devotionem ad sanctum Sebastianum habere."[9] The attempts of artists to accommodate both views are of interest not only to the art historian but to the historian of ideas; here as in so many other areas of medieval thought, art and literature provide complementary expressions of the same social attitudes. In this paper I should like to trace the gradual development of plague imagery in medieval art, with special attention to the contributions of scientific and religious thought concerning the origins of the disease.

Medieval artists, especially manuscript painters, were a conservative lot. They preferred to adapt a familiar image to a new context rather than to create something new. This had been true in early appropriations from classical culture such as the use of Hercules or Orpheus as figure types for Sampson or Christ.[10] It also held true in the fifteenth century, when the rise of an urban bourgeoisie with a taste for illuminated manuscripts led to a striking increase in the production of modestly illustrated books, and especially of books of hours.[11] To help speed the making of such books, the craftsmen in ateliers often used model books, which, of course, encouraged the borrowing or adapting of preexisting forms or themes to express recent social phenomena.

Sometimes the older models were simply inadequate to express

the new subject matter. For example, in a manuscript of Boccaccio's *Decameron* dating from the end of the fourteenth century,[12] the
illustrations for the Prologue, describing the coming of the plague
to Florence, are all borrowed from other forms of art. Although
Boccaccio was at great pains to describe the epidemic in realistic
detail, the illustrator provides only a kind of visual shorthand (fig.
1). The sequence begins with a flying Death holding a scythe and
regarding some bodies; it then shows us a sick man's chamber, probably taken from Boethius illustration; finally, there is a funeral procession, borrowed from the Office for the Dead in a book of hours.
Each element of this gentle, backward-looking sequence was to un-
dergo change in the hands of later artists. The changes, however,
were subtle, involving a shift of emphasis rather than complete abandonment of the original image. Thus the personified Death and
the funeral procession remain key elements in the depiction of the
plague in the fifteenth century, but they are rendered differently.

Consider how Chaucer, in the *Pardoner's Tale*, describes the disease. Its protagonists, three blasphemous young men, are drink-
ing in a Flemish[13] tavern when:

> ... they herde a belle clynke
> Biforn a cors, was caried to his grave.

They ask whose corpse it is, and learn that it is that of an old companion, slain by:

> ... a privee theef men clepeth Deeth,
> That in this contree al the peple sleeth,
> And with his spere he smoot his herte atwo,
> And wente his way withouten wordes mo.
> He hath a thousand slayn this pestilence.[14]

The first image, that of the outdoor funeral procession with its clink-
ing bell, was an all too common sight during the plague years. Early
fourteenth-century depictions of funerals were apt to dwell upon
the ceremony within the church with the pall-draped coffin subor-
dinated to the officiants[15] as in an initial from a horae in Keble
College, Oxford (fig. 2). Here an acolyte, and priest with book,
pray over the coffin.[16] Illustrations for the Office of the Dead[17]
after the middle of the century begin to show the coffin in motion
on its way to the burial place. The change in these scenes during
the fifteenth century has been well described by Erwin Panofsky,

who noted that "in the illustration of the Vigils for the Dead, the gruesomeness of the cemetery came to be substituted for the solemnity of a church service."[18] These later illustrations generally show the coffin on its way to or at the place of burial, as in a scene of a procession going from church to churchyard, from a horae in the Municipal Library of Poitiers (fig. 3). Already the grave is being dug in the foreground and old bones lie here and there on the grass to remind the viewer of what will become of the body. In another such scene from the *Très belles heures* (fig. 4), the graveyard has now completely replaced the church; the body is now a skeleton and the *membra disjecta* of other corpses show what will become of it. No doubt Chaucer's familiarity with such burials in real life as in art is reflected in the *Pardoner's Tale*.

Chaucer's personified Death pierces his victim's heart with a spear. We are accustomed to think of the grim reaper's attribute as the scythe shown in the Boccaccio miniature, and this seems to have been his standard attribute before 1348. Cesarius of Heisterbach, for example, notes that "certain people think that death is a person … in the form of a man with a scythe."[19] Thus Chaucer's Death seems a more aggressive personification, and well it might. The mortality brought on by the plague was on so vast a scale that it would have been difficult for an observer of it to think of death as anything less than aggressive. The spear, however, results from a subtle development in the iconography of death which also began with the coming of the plague. After 1348 the familiar scythe was quickly replaced by a spear, or when the personification was at a considerable distance from the victim, by an arrow.[20] This new imagery can be seen in a miniature from the Office for the Dead from the *Très riches heures* (fig. 5) where a row of corpses in military formation advance before an army of living men. The painter, Jean Colombe, has placed only one scythe among their spears and other thrusting weapons.[21]

Most contemporary accounts agreed that the plague came from Asia.[22] An anonymous chronicler of Flanders reported that the disease started east of India, when storms raged for three days. On the first day, frogs, snakes, lizards and scorpions rained from the skies. On the second came thunder, lightning and huge hail stones which caused an enormous mortality. On the third day came a stinking fire and smoke, which killed most of the remaining men and beasts and burnt up all the cities. The whole province was attacked by these storms and the infection was carried by a stinking wind to the coast.[23] In this early account can be seen the atmospheric and miasmal theories of the plague's origins which were to be more fully developed in the treatises prepared by the medical community.

How the plague traveled westward from its somewhat mythic starting point was recounted by Gabriel de Mussis, a Piacenzan notary whose *Historia de morbo* gave an eyewitness account of the disease in Italy. He writes that a Genoese trading station in the Crimean, named Tana, the modern port of Azov, was besieged in 1343 by Mongols, who suddenly began to die of a mysterious illness. Among the defenders were certain Italian merchants who fled to Kaffa, the modern Russian Feodosiya, another Genoese mercantile settlement in the Crimean. The pagans, following the fugitives, besieged that town in turn, but the plague also followed the besiegers, and in metaphors which we shall see in a number of treatments of the Black Death, "thousands died as if arrows from heaven were striking them down and abasing their pride. Thus everywhere men felt the blow of the bitter arrow which brings sudden death. So widespread and so great was this general mortality that men suspected the extreme judgment of God upon them."[24] Another chronicler, Giovanni Villani, added that the judgment was manifested by subterranean and celestial fires, and that a great number of locusts, both living and dead, fell upon the countryside and poisoned it.[25] Eventually the Italian merchants, fleeing Kaffa, took ship for Constantinople and from there to Genoa, Venice, and other Christian ports, bringing the plague everywhere they landed. Taking on for the moment the persona of these merchants and sailors, de Mussis exclaims "our ships came to port, but of a thousand sailors, barely 10 survive. We reach our homes and our kin come to greet us, but woe to us, for we cast at them the arrows of death. While we spoke to them, while they kissed and embraced us, we scattered poison from our lips."[26]

The idea that the plague had been sent as some form of divine retribution was a natural one. As Philipa Tristram points out:

> the suddenness of the onslaught, the arbitrariness with which it struck, the impossibility of explaining in any sort of rational way how the infection was carried, led to the supposition that the disease was the instrument of divine vengeance.[27]

Divine vengeance made concrete in military images had a long tradition. Exod. 8–11 contains a variety of them; in *Iliad* I.44–52, Apollo sends arrows of plague upon the Greeks and in Macrobius' *Saturnalia* (book 1, chap. 17) a statue of Apollo is described holding arrows of the plague in his left hand and curative graces in his right.

Responses to the Black Death offered by clerics and canonists such as Bartolus de Saxoferrato, who argued that "the plague is a direct act of war or enmity on the part of God against the human race,"[28] embodied such imagery. In art a representative exemplification of God's wrath in the guise of an arrow or spear symbolizing the plague[29] can be seen in a woodcut from a German *pestblätt* or plague leaflet advertising a church or saint's shrine where miracles were believed to take place (fig. 6). These flyers were hawked by pedlars from town to town and often used by their buyers to decorate walls and help avert the disease. Such scenes figure the response of pious men to an inexplicable disaster in their lives and offer an objective form for their fears.

The medico-astrological explanation of the plague at first competed with the supernatural one, as we see in Boccaccio's description in the *Decameron* of the Black Death at Florence. "The plague started in the east," he said, "either because of God's just anger or through the influence of the heavenly bodies on men."[30] What exactly this influence was can best be seen in the "official" explanation for the disease, issued by the medical faculty of the University of Paris in 1348 at the request of Phillip VI of France. This treatise, the *Compendium de Epidemia*, explained that:

> the remote and first cause of the plague was a planetary conjunction which took place on March 20, 1345, at one o'clock in the afternoon in the sign of Aquarius.[31]

The treatise goes on to cite Aristotle and Albert the Great to the effect that a conjunction of Saturn, Jupiter and Mars in a warm and humid sign led to the poisoning of the earth's atmosphere, for corrupt vapors were drawn up from land and sea and intermixed by violent winds with the very substance of the air itself. The authors also, in a burst of chauvinism, suggest that the great winds much remarked on during this period brought to France pestilential vapors from the marshes and from unburied bodies found in other countries.[32]

The miasmic explanation of the plague's cause was very popular with later physicians and writers of plague tracts. Raymond
Chalmel de Viviers, an influential physician from the papal court
at Avignon, in book one of his *De peste*, spoke of the plague her-
alded by a "heaviness of the heavens, many thick clouds obscuring
moon and stars, while the sun grew pale and men smelt an impure
air."[33] The Paduan physician, Galeazzo di Santa Sofia, attributed
the impurity to a vast number of locusts falling into the sea and
rotting there.[34] Putridity as a concrete embodiment of the miasmal
theory appears in the *De Signis* of Jacob Mennel, court astrologer
and genealogist to Maximilian I. This book contains entries for
many celestial events with indications that they were accompanied
by various maladies. Mennel's miniature (fig. 7) shows the sky full
of locusts and other vermin giving off evil vapors. According to
the accompanying text, the dense cloud of locusts had passed from
east to west, darkening the heavens and destroying the crops, and
from the rotting of their bodies came a horrible pestilence.[35]

Most accounts describing ways of avoiding the plague, from the
counsels of the *Compendium* onward, stressed in one way or another
its airborne nature. John Lydgate's *Doctrine for the Pestilence*, a Middle English poetic restatement of the *Compendium's consilia*, advised
men:

> Who will been holle & kepe hym from sekenesse
> And resiste the strok of pestilence,
> Lat hym be glad, & voide al hevynesse,
> Flee wikkyd heires, eschew the presence
> Off infect placys....
> Walk in cleene heir, eschew mystis blake.[36]

If avoidance was not practical, then the creation of one's own,
healthier atmosphere was counselled through the use of pomander
balls and amber apples for the rich,[37] and for the poor, smoulder-
ing juniper, ash and pine. Indeed, the perfume industry owes its
start to the plague, as does the familiar eau de Cologne,[38] used
in that city to mask the smell of the sick and protect the healthy
from airborne disease. A woodcut from John Ketham's *Fasciculus
Medicinae* portrays these methods of countering the danger of mi-
asma. In the room of a dying plague victim (fig. 8) a physician
smells a pomander ball while he takes the patient's pulse and his

less fortunate attendants content themselves with a basket of burning herbs and a torch.[39]

The *Compendium*, a Latin treatise with an involved scholastic structure, was quickly popularized in an anonymous French prose version of 1350,[40] and in a poetic rendering by Olivier de la Haye made in 1426.[41] It was also epitomized in German by Heinrich Mügeln, d. 1371, at the court of Charles IV in Prague.[42] Though the original Latin text paid only lip service to the idea that God's anger had caused the disease — for the physicians obviously preferred the astrological explanation — la Haye's translation, which had numerous expansions and interpolations, tried to accommodate both ideas by having the conjunction decreed by a council of planetary deities in response to God's wishes.

In this, he was following an elaborate poem on the great planetary conjunction, *De Judicio Solis in Conviviis Saturni*, written in 1350 by a Liègois canon, Simon of Couvin. The poem describes an assembly of the gods convoked by Saturn. Jupiter and Saturn, who represent antithetical attitudes towards mankind, quarrel, Saturn proposing reasons for mankind's destruction and Jupiter coming to its defense. Sol judges between them with Mercury serving as the clerk of the court. Mercury notes that the plague comes from God on account of the sins of humanity, just as did Noah's flood. Since mankind's present sins are greater than its antediluvian ones, Sol decrees a correspondingly more horrific punishment and entrusts the three planets of the conjunction with carrying out the sentence. Saturn then causes thick and heavy rainless clouds to suffocate Juno, or the lower air, which becomes corrupt and poisons mankind.[43]

As can be seen from this synopsis, Olivier de la Haye and Simon of Couvin were not completely comfortable with a purely astrological and determinist explanation for the disease, and wished to reconcile the pietist and medical viewpoints. Simon's poem, especially, seems to have been intended in part to counter clerical objections to the *Compendium*, which was attacked in a number of sermons. Thomas Brinton (1320–1389), bishop of Rochester and one of the most famous preachers of his age, in a sermon dealing with the plague, castigated "those who ascribe it to certain planets and constellations." Showing his familiarity with Simon's poem, he observes:

since the corruption of lust and the designs of wickedness
are greater today than in Noah's time — for a thousand forms
of vice are practiced today which did not exist then — let us
not impute the scourges of God to planets but rather to our
sins.[44]

A visual image that brought together, in some measure, the astrological and pietist viewpoints was that of the comet.[45] Though
comets were often seen as the cause of the disease — for example
one treatise stated succinctly that "cometa stella est ... in cujus or-
tis pesti" (B.N. Lat. 6885, fol. 27) — they were also phenomena in
the natural world which indicated God's anger. *Diues et Pauper*, a
Middle English dialogue written between 1405 and 1410 contains
a formulation of this attitude. Diues, a well-to-do bourgeois, questions Pauper, a poor but learned friar:

> ... telle me ʒyf þe wondrys þat fallyn aʒens kende in þe
> bodyis abouyn betokenyn ... ony auenturis þat been com-
> yngge. *Pauper.* Þat fallyʒt aʒens comoun cours of kende be-
> tokenyʒt þat sumthyng is comyngge pasyng comoun cours of
> kende ... comounly sueche wondrys fallyn more aʒens woo
> þan aʒens wele, as cometys ... been tokenys þat þe peple qhere
> þey apperyn doon aʒens kende and þat lord of al nature is
> offendyd wyt hem and alle creaturis, redy to punyshyn hem.
> *Diues.* It may wel been as þu seyst, for manye sueche han ap-
> peryd wytinne a fewe ʒerys, neuere, I trowe, so manye in so
> lytil qhyle, and mechil sorwe and woo folwyʒt after, as we
> felyn, heryn, and seen. But, I preye þe qhat betokenede þat
> wondyrful comete ... queche apperydde [in] MCCCII? *Pauper.*
> It was opyn tokene of þe grete offens of God wyth þe peple
> of Engelond and þat hard wreche was comynge but þey
> wolden amenden hem of here falshed and ... oþer synnys
> many mo.... *Diues.* What seyn clerkes of sweche cometis?...
> *Pauper.* They seyn that whenne it appereth it signefieth
> moreyn....[46]

The comet, which had been associated with the plague since antiquity, was easily seen as a cause of corrupt atmosphere as well
as an evil omen. Most medieval comet lore derived from their treatment as portents in Manilius' *Astronomica*,[47] and from the elabo-

rate account of the different types and colors of comets and their
Arabic names in the spurious final paragraph of Ptolemy's *Centi-loquium*.[48] It was a rare chronicle of the plague years that did not
include a comet as a portent of things to come, and as we shall
see, some medical writers tried to show a causal connection between comets and the epidemic.

Typical of those who saw comets as ill omens was Henri of Ferrières, who, in the *Livre du Roy Modus*, described a prophetic vision he had had in which the Holy Spirit sent war, famine and
plague upon humanity for its sins. These afflictions, he said, would
be portended by heavenly signs: an eclipse when the sun entered
the constellation of the Lion, and the appearance of a comet of the
type which, according to Ptolemy, brought great plagues upon
mankind.[49]

Exactly how comets affected the lives of men and brought the
plague was, as we might expect, explained by several physicians
and writers on the Black Death. Basing his thought partly on Aristotle's statement in *Meteorologica* I.7 that comets dry the body and
so cause an abundance of choler, resulting in a propensity for strife,
Raymond Chalmel de Viviers saw comets as causes of the plague
itself. In the chapters of his *De peste* devoted to astral causes, he
observed that "in times of plague, comets are seen, whose burning
shapes fly through the air, which they vitiate. In turn, the humours
of our bodies are corrupted and the plague is induced."[50] The hot
nature of comets and their drying effects on man's atmosphere was
portrayed by Hans Folz, whose plague verses of 1482 explain that:

> comets with fiery tails are known in Germany
> as drying stars because they withdraw
> all moisture from the places over which they fly.
> This may be seen by the great plague
> and this too is a cause of corrupt atmosphere.[51]

That comets cause droughts which bring the plague in their train
is an idea shown in the text and accompanying miniature of Mennel's *De Signis*. The entry for the year 1412, based on an actual
outbreak of plague in Silesia[52] that year, is illustrated by a picture
(fig. 9) showing comets in the shapes of peacock tails; they appeared
in January of 1412 and brought plague to the west. Hardly had
one comet passed, Mennel notes, than another came, inflicting a
heavy mortality. In the next year, an incredible drought followed,
and pestilence. Treatises like Mennel's, however, seem to have ap-

pealed more to learned than to popular audiences.

Popular piety most frequently expressed itself in the image of the intercessor saint as a point of contact between a wrathful God and man. The rise in the cult of such saints is perhaps the most simple and direct response to the disease which we can observe in medieval art.[53] In the hope of averting or tempering God's anger, medieval men and women prayed to a variety of figures, of whom three, the Virgin, and saints Sebastian and Roch are particularly common in medieval art.

Prayers to the Virgin for protection from the plague were very popular. The poems of John Lydgate on this theme may be taken as representative. In one piece, he asks her to "... Pray / Thy swete son ... / That no perylous plage of pestilence ... / Entyr in England...."[54] In another lyric, he again shows his familiarity with the *Compendium de Epidemia*, begging her:

> ... do not now disdeyne
> Contraryous planetis to Appeese & Represse,
> Whos dredefull werrys do men full Mortall peyne,
> Be vnholsome Eyres Cawsyng greete sykenesse.[55]

A scene of the Virgin protecting people from the arrows of God's wrath appears in an altarpiece from the Church of the Carmelites at Göttingen[56] (fig. 10). Here she extends her mantle over them to ward off the arrows directed at them by the Father. In spite of the figurative nature of the scene, the painter is quite realistic, placing the arrows in spots traditionally the sites of buboes in plague victims.

As we learn from de Mussis, "bitter blows vexed the flesh of those who caught the disease. A certain cold rigor came on the body as if it were pierced by lances or struck by arrows. And in the armpit or the groin, between the skin and the body, in the fashion of a very hard fig, came an awful swelling, whose heat brought an acute fever with headache."[57] It is these swellings, the buboes, which gave the lymphatic form of the disease its name.[58] One appears on the thigh of Saint Roch (fig. 11), modestly moved there from its actual home in the groin, in a fifteenth-century book of hours now in London.[59] The arrows of the plague imagined as crossbow bolts strike both in the lymph nodes of the neck, and in the groin of a figure in the posture of Saint Roch in a Swabian panel painting done in 1510, now in the Munich Pinothek, and entitled *The Plague* (fig. 12).

Because the arrow was so widely used as an image of the plague, it was natural that those seeking protection from the disease should also turn to saints Sebastian and Roch. The former's martyrdom under a hail of arrows — from which he did not die — was a favorite subject of medieval art and devotional literature. Suffrages or prayers to individual saints, which make up part of many fifteenth- and sixteenth-century horae contain his portrait and various invocations,[60] of which this example from the York horae will indicate their averting character.

> Sancte Sebastiane
> ....
> Protege me et conserua
> et a me, martyr, enerua
> infirmitatem noxiam,
> vocatam epidemiam
> ....
> Tu ...
> hanc pestilentiam, si vis,
> potes facere cessare,
> et a Deo impetare.[61]

Sometimes Sebastian is shown interceding with God directly on behalf of plague sufferers, as he does in a painting by Josse Lieferinxe.[62] The boil on the neck of the dying man in the left foreground adds to the immediacy of the scene (fig. 13). In fifteenth-century Umbrian paintings, Sebastian commonly replaces the Virgin as protector of the city; arrows break harmlessly on his outstretched mantle.[63]

Sebastian, who was martyred in the third century, was an established saint at the time of the first outbreak of the Black Death in 1348. His role as an intercessor against the plague was based more on the symbolism of the arrow — he was the patron of archers and crossbowmen — than on any experience he himself had had with the disease.[64] Saint Roch, however, was born about 1350 and contracting the plague, recovered from it. In 1379, while on a pilgrimage during which he cured plague victims, he was imprisoned as a spy near Montpellier and there he died.[65] Evidence of a fully developed cult of Roch appears as early as 1413 in a confraternity in his honor at Clermont-l'Herault.[66] And on occasion, he too, appears in suffrages. A prayer in the York horae asks "O beate confessor Roche, quam magna apud Deum sunt merita tua, quibus credimus nos a morbo epidemie posse liberari, et aeris temperiem concedi."[67]

Chantry guilds or confraternities in honor of Sebastian and Roch were a common feature of late medieval life.[68] Lay persons, often members of the same trade guilds, banded together to provide masses for the good of their souls after death and for protection from the pestilence during their lives. These confraternities, whose liturgical activities were somewhat similar to those of the private chantry chapels founded by the wealthy and ministered to by paid priests or chaplains,[69] provide us with many images of these saints, usually in wood sculpture, wall painting and stained glass.

With the waning interest in a universal last judgment after Benedict XII's edict of 1336 establishing individual judgment of souls, there grew up in founders of chantry chapels and members of confraternities alike a marked interest in prayers and masses for souls in purgatory and other measures by which prayers to patron saints might benefit the souls of living and dead. For an idea of the claims made in Roch's name, we may look at the text of another *pestblätt* of the late fifteenth century in the Braunschweig State Library, advertising a celebration at the Church of the Carmelites in Paris.

> The day after the Assumption of the Virgin will be celebrated the feast of the glorious friend of God, Saint Roch, true preserver from the plague, where his confraternity will receive from the bishop of Paris, the Cardinal de Gurce and other cardinals, 100 days of true pardon.

The flyer goes on to promise certain pleasures for the eye and ear as well as salvation for the soul.

> A very handsome and rich reliquary engraved with pictures of Saint Roch will be shown in the church of the Carmelites on the day of the feast and on the same day in the morning and afternoon will be recited a sermon by a doctor in theology and the saint's miracles will be declared.[70]

Sebastian had much the same cult following. The archers' guilds of France donated many windows with inscriptions asking Sebastian "to protect fellow archers from the plague,"[71] and a wealthy merchant, Sebastian Turbil, who recovered from the disease, established a chapel honoring his name saint at Lanslevillard in

Savoie. It contained seventeen frescoes of episodes in the life of
the saint; one of these shows a doctor cauterizing a bubo while a
good angel restrains a devil from sending an arrow of plague upon
the community.[72] This fresco is unusual in its combination of medical and pietistic material in a single image.

Both Roch and Sebastian appear, as well, on plague pence and
tokens designed to avert the disease. On the face of one such coin
from Poland, formerly in the Countway Medical Library, Harvard, we find an inscription, "signum Rochi contra pestem pa-
tronus." Though this coin dates from 1707,[73] similar examples exist from the first quarter of the sixteenth century in Germany.[74]
It is likely that such coins developed with the rise of Roch's cult
in the early fifteenth century. That Sebastian must also have been
featured on similar coins and tokens is shown by his association
with them in a scene from his martyrdom in the Soane Hours in
London,[75] ca. 1500 (fig. 14). The artist apparently looked at such
coins in order to paint the trompe-l'oeil borders.

We know from chronicles of the period that amulets, prayers
and pomander balls were of no avail to the thousands who suc-
cumbed to the disease. The anonymous chronicler of Flanders,
writing not long after the outbreak of the plague, tells of the report
of a friend in the train of a cardinal on a visit to the curia at Avignon. Within the walls of the city, his friend observed, more than
seven thousand houses were uninhabited, and in a certain field just
consecrated by the pope as an emergency cemetery, 11,000 bodies
were buried.[76] Artists seem to have taken such mass burials as a
universal image of the plague's impact, as we can see from several
representations in manuscript painting.

In a late fifteenth-century French horae, now in Copenhagen,[77]
a scene from the Office for the Dead gives many of the elements
of the iconographic tradition we have been examining (fig. 15).
At the top, an exterminating angel waves his unsheathed sword.
He is accompanied by the rubric "La grande peste et mortalitie."
Below in registers at the sides of the text are corpse bearers, at the
bottom the sick and dying, and in the lower right a carter bearing
away bodies has himself fallen victim to the disease. This miniature is probably based on scenes in which Saint Gregory, in a procession of plague victims, caused a similar angel on Hadrian's tomb
to sheathe his sword (fig. 16).[78] Two miniatures from a horae in
Paris (figs. 17 and 18) show the soul of the plague victim carried

to the heavens, while the body with darkened complexion and buboes realistically portrayed lies below the column of text and a group of victims display their sores. Feet and hats in the receding background show the extent of the epidemic.

Typically, these burial scenes stress not only the number of the dead, but also the inability of the living to cope with these numbers. In plague burial scenes such as the well-known example in the second *Chronicle* of Gilles li Muisis, abbot of St. Martin's, Tornai,[79] (fig. 19) number is indicated by frantic and repetitive activity. A similar miniature from the *Très belles heures* (fig. 20) shows by their workaday and unceremonious nature the frequency of such burials, and the exterminating angel above indicates the cause of death.

That there were not more objective and descriptive images of plague victims in medieval art may be owing to the causes mentioned earlier. First, the pictorial expression of the medico-astrological view of the disease with its strong ties to the medical profession and its verbalization in the *Compendium de Epidemia* was quickly replaced by images of a more fearful sort which substituted a preventive agent — most often a saint — for the patient to be cured, or by gloomy but general ones of burials of various kinds in which death is regarded as a subject for contemplation. Second, there was a preexisting artistic vocabulary by which to present the impact of the plague. Of the images to which medieval men turned, the signs and portents of the Black Death such as comets, an angry God shooting arrows at the earth, and intercessor saints — only those of the cemetery and of the grave in which the corpse rather than the coffin is shown developed after 1348. The others were well-established before the Black Death: saints' lives since the early years of Christianity and celestial portents since antiquity, while the arrows sent by God may have existed in Byzantine illustrative programs for the *Iliad*. Such a preexisting vocabulary, though it may not have exactly fitted the circumstances of the plague, was already available, useful, and accordingly, may have hindered the development of a more specific and graphic set of images. And finally, people may have found direct visual confrontation of the disease in art too unpleasant, difficult or frightening and preferred to focus their attention on peripheral matters. Indeed, li Muisis says in his poem on the plague as he describes the mourning everywhere around him, "I don't wish to say anymore about it, for it is far better to be quiet than to give other details."[80]

Knowing as we do the conservative nature of medieval manuscript illustration we should not be surprised to find artists copy-
ing or adapting old pictures even while writers of the period such
as Boccaccio or Gabriel de Mussis were attempting to describe the
Black Death as they saw it around them. The very slow appearance of new plague imagery in art is, moreover, a function of the
means of transmission in an age when books were rare, expensive,
and laboriously produced by hand. The coming of the printing
press and the rise of the woodcut were to change all of that, but
in the years before 1448, graves outnumbered books; it seems fitting that some of the earliest artistic innovation resulting from the
plague should appear in the Office for the Dead in books of hours
and in the suffrages for the intercessor saints. These images are
indirect evidence of how men responded to the plague, of course,
but they speak to us in place of more direct scenes of sickrooms
and planetary schemata which seem never to have seized the popular imagination in the Middle Ages.

Notes

I am grateful to the officials of the Countway Medical Library, Harvard,
to Susan Alon of the Yale University Medical Library and to K. Gaylord,
W. G. Land, M. Malvern and E. Schifferl for aid and information.

1. The bibliography of the plague is vast, but among the most useful studies
are Anna Campbell, *The Black Death and Men of Learning* (New York, 1931);
Johannes Nohl, *The Black Death: A Chronicle of the Plague, compiled from Contemporary Sources*, trans. C. H. Clarke (London, 1961); Charles Creighton, *A History of Epidemics in Britain*, 2nd ed. (London, 1965); George Deaux, *The Black
Death, 1347* (New York, 1969); J. F. D. Shrewsbury, *A History of Bubonic
Plague in the British Isles* (Cambridge, 1970); Michael W. Dols, *The Black Death
in the Middle East* (Princeton, 1977); and Robert Gottfried, *Epidemic Disease
in Fifteenth Century England* (New Brunswick, 1978).

2. Jean-Noël Biraben, *Les hommes et la peste en France et dans les pays européens
et méditerranéens*, 2 vols. (Paris and The Hague, 1975–1976). See also Carl von
Mayer, *Die Pest in Bildern aus der Vergangenheit* (St. Petersburg, 1879); Millard
Meiss, *Painting in Florence and Siena after the Black Death* (Princeton, 1951); and

Louis Edward Jordan, "The Iconography of Death in Western Medieval Art to 1350" (Ph.D. diss., University of Notre Dame, 1980).

3. See particularly, Raymond Crawford, *The Plague and Pestilence in Literature and Art* (Oxford, 1914) and Henri H. Mollaret and Jacqueline Brossollet, *La peste, source méconnue d'inspiration artistique* (Antwerp, 1965) who say that the Dance of Death "découla directement de la peste," p. 69. See generally on the Dance of Death Rudolf Helm, *Skelett- und Todesdarstellungen bis zum Auftreten der Totentänze* (Strassburg, 1928); Stephan Kozáky, *Geschichte der Totentänze* (Budapest, 1936); Ethel C. Williams, "The Dance of Death in Painting and Sculpture in the Middle Ages," *Journal of the British Archaeological Association*, 3rd ser. 1 (1937): 229–57; James M. Clark, *The Dance of Death in the Middle Ages and the Renaissance* (Glasgow, 1950); Hellmut Rosenfeld, *Der mittelalterliche Totentänz* (Cologne, 1954); Kathi Mayer-Baer, *The Music of the Spheres and the Dance of Death* (Princeton, 1970); Joël Saugnieux, *Les danses macabres de France et d'Espagne* (Lyon, 1971); and R. Hammerstein, *Tanz und Musik des Todes: Die mittelalterlichen Totentänze und ihr nachleben* (Bern and Munich, 1980).

4. On this motif, see the forthcoming study by William G. Land of the Cloisters prayerbook of Bonne of Luxembourg.

5. See Erwin Panofsky, *Tomb Sculpture* (New York, 1960), pp. 56, 63; H. s'Jacob, *Idealism and Realism: A Study of Sepulchral Symbolism* (Leiden, 1954), p. 46; Ernst Kantorowicz, *The King's Two Bodies* (Princeton, 1957), pp. 432–35; and Kathleen Cohen, *Metamorphosis of a Death Symbol, The Transi Tomb in the Late Middle Ages and the Renaissance* (Berkeley, 1973), p. 4.

6. I have found no connection between the plague and the motif of the Three Living and the Three Dead. Dance of Death poetry, which shows Death leading off members of various estates, frequently contains a general speech by Death to mankind. Here is an example from the fifteenth-century *La danza de la muerte*, ed. T. A. Sánchez and J. Pidal, *Biblioteca de autores españoles*, vol. 57 (Madrid, 1921), p. 179, "what manifest insanity is this to think that others will die and you alone will survive. In fact, you cannot be certain whether in some inconvenient moment will come upon you some corruption from a morbid swelling of the glands or a red pustule." Much the same material occurs in John Lydgate's verses on the Dance of Death fresco once in St. Paul's Churchyard. See Eleanor Hammond, *English Verse Between Chaucer and Surrey* (Durham, N.C., 1927), p. 131. Here, the unexpected appearance of the plague is designed to discourage human vanity; other equally inconvenient modes of death could be substituted to make the same point. Also to be found in these poems is a stanza in which the Physician as a representative of his estate admits that all his learning about the pestilence will not stave off Death. In the hours of Notre Dame, fol. 100, once in the Rothschild Collection, a physician holds a urinoscopy flask while Death parodies his gesture. See Pierre de Nesson, *Pierre de Nesson et ses oeuvres*, ed. A. Piaget and E. Droz (Paris, 1925), p. 108. See also Alberto Tenenti, *La vie et mort à travers l'art du XVe siècle* (Paris, 1952), pp. 28–29, and A. S. Warthin, "The Physician of the Dance of Death," *Annals of Medical History* 2 (1930): 351–71, 453–69, 697–710. On the whole tradition of the Dance and the estates, see André Corvoisier, "Représentations de la société dans les danses des morts, XVe-XVIIIe siècles," *Revue*

92 Iconography of the plague

d'histoire moderne et contemporaine 4 (1969): 489–535.

7. One exception to this statement is the "Debate Between the Body and the Worms" (B.L. MS Additional 37049), in which a transi tomb provides a setting for the dialogue. The work begins "In þe ceson of huge mortalite / Of sondre disseses with þe pestilence / Heuely reynand whilom in cuntre" (fol. 33r). The speaker is impelled by the times to go on a pilgrimage and enters a church where he sees a transi tomb, but there is no further connection with the plague. See on this work, Marjorie Malvern, "An Earnest 'monyscyon' and 'þinge delectabyll' Realized Verbally and Visually in 'A Disputacion betwyx þe Body and Wormes,'" A Middle English Poem inspired by Tomb Art and Northern Spirituality," *Viator* 13 (1982): 425–43, and generally, Susan Powell and Alan Fletcher, " 'In die sepulture seu trigintali': The Late Medieval Funeral and Memorial Sermon," *Leeds Studies in English* 12 (1981): 195–228; as well as Pamela M. King, "Eight English *Memento Mori* Verses from Cadaver Tombs," *N&Q* 226 (1981): 494–96.

8. Meiss, *Painting in Florence*, pp. 75–77.

9. Felix J. H. Skene, ed., *Liber Pluscardensis*, vol. 1, book 9, chap. 40 (Edinburgh, 1877).

10. See John Block Friedman, *Orpheus in the Middle Ages* (Cambridge, Mass., 1970), pp. 39–40.

11. See, for example, L. J. M. Delaissé, "The Importance of Books of Hours for the History of the Medieval Book," in *Gatherings in Honor of Dorothy Miner* (Baltimore, 1974), pp. 212–13.

12. The scene is briefly discussed by Tenenti, *La vie et la mort*, p. 35.

13. It is appropriate that Chaucer chose Flanders for the setting, for a rather large number of our literary and artistic records of the plague come from that region.

14. Geoffrey Chaucer, *The Works of Geoffrey Chaucer*, ed. F. N. Robinson (Boston, 1957), lines 664–65, 675–79. The brevity of Chaucer's treatment has been remarked on by Shrewsbury, *A History*, p. 41. See also Peter G. Beidler, "The Plague and Chaucer's Pardoner," *The Chaucer Review* 16 (1982): 257–69, and, more generally, S. Wenzel, "Pestilence and Middle English Literature: Friar John Grimstone's Poems on Death" in *The Black Death: The Impact of the Fourteenth-Century Plague* ed. Daniel Williman, Medieval & Renaissance Texts & Studies, vol. 13 (Binghamton, 1982): 131–59; and H. Braet and W. Verbelse eds. *Death in the Middle Ages* (Louvain, 1983).

15. See Millard Meiss, "La mort et l'office des morts à l'epoque du Mâitre de Boucicaut et des Limbourg," *Revue de l'art* 1 (1968): 17.

16. This miniature is discussed by M. B. Parkes, *The Medieval Manuscripts of Keble College, Oxford* (London, 1979), p. 45.

17. See for example B.L. MS Additional 27697, fol. 194, ca. 1460.

18. Erwin Panofsky, *Early Netherlandish Painting*, vol. 1 (Cambridge, Mass., 1964), p. 74.

19. Cesarius Heisterbacensis, *Dialogus Miraculorum*, ed. Joseph Strange, vol. 2 (Cologne, 1851), p. 312.

20. The best study of the arrow's connection with the plague and with Saint Sebastian is that of Paul Perdrizet, *La vierge de miséricorde* (Paris, 1908), pp.

107–49 passim. For more recent discussion, see Meiss, *Painting in Florence*, p. 77 and Philippa Tristram, *Figures of Life and Death in Medieval English Literature* (New York, 1976), p. 177.

21. See Benjamin Bord, "Six images des *Très riches heures*," *Sudhoff's Mitteilungen Geschichte der Medizin und Naturwissenschaft* 31 (1932): 185.

22. See generally Biraben, *Les hommes et la peste*, 1:50 and Dols, *The Black Death*, pp. 52–54.

23. J. J. de Smet, ed., "Breve Chronicon Clerici Anonymi," in *Receuil des chroniques de Flandres*, vol. 3 (Brussels 1837–1865), p. 14.

24. Gabriel de Mussis, *Ystoria de morbo*, ed. A. W. Henschel, "Document zur Geschichte des schwarzen Todes," *Archiv für die gesammte Medizin* 2 (1842): 48–49. On this author, see Vincent J. Derbes, "De Mussis and the Great Plague of 1348," *Journal of the American Medical Association*, vol. 196, no. 1 (1966): 179–82.

25. Giovanni Villani, *Croniche di Giovanni Villani*, ed. A. Racheli, vol. 1, book 12, chap. 84 (Trieste, 1857), p. 492.

26. Gabriel de Mussis, *Ystoria de morbo*, p. 50.

27. Tristram, *Figures of Life and Death*, p. 8.

28. Bartolus of Saxoferrato, Commentary on *Digests* 37.13.1, *Opera*, vol. 4, 171ʳ (Basel, 1588–1589). This also may relate to *Decretals* II, c. 16, q. 1, cap. 65.

29. This *pestblätt* is published and discussed in Paul Heitz and W. L. Schreiber, *Pestblätter des XV Jahrhunderts* (Strassburg, 1901), p. 3. On the three arrows as symbolizing war, famine and plague, see Perdrizet, *La vierge*, p. 135.

30. Giovanni Boccaccio, *Il Decameron*, ed. Charles S. Singleton, vol. 1, Prologue (Bari, 1955).

31. *Compendium de Epidemia*, ed. H. Emile Rébouis, *Étude historique et critique sur la peste*, part 1, chap. 1 (Paris, 1888), pp. 76–80; chap. 2, p. 82. On the *Compendium*, see also Campbell, *The Black Death and Men of Learning*; Biraben, *Les hommes*, 1:133 and 2:9–10; and Dols, *The Black Death*, p. 40.

32. Dols cites an extraordinarily similar Arabic explanation for the disease from Ibn an-Nafis' commentary on Avicenna, p. 88.

33. Raymond Chalmel de Viviers, *De peste*, book 1, chap. 4 in *Libri Tres Opera Iacobi Dalechampi* (Lugduni, 1553), p. 50.

34. Galeazzo di Santa Sofia, *De Febribus Tractatus*, in *Opus Aureum* (Venice, 1517), chap. 1, fol. 169ᵛ. The third of the seven signs predicting the plague given by Jean Jasme, a fourteenth-century Provençal physician was "quant nous voions sus la terre au temps deste abundance de mouches. Et ce signe denote infection de lair," *Remede tres utile contra fievre pestilencieuse* (Paris, 1481), sig. A.1 and A.1ᵛ. On this author, see Ernst Wickersheimer, "Jehan Jacme (Joannes Jacobi) et les régimes de pestilence qui portent son nom," *Archivio di storia della scienza* 6 (1925): 105–12.

35. On Mennel, see A. Lhotsky, "Dr. Jacob Mennel, ein Vorarlberger im Kreise Kaiser Maximilians I," *Alemannia. Zeitschrift für Geschichte, Heimat-und Volkskunde Vorarlbergs*, vol. 10, n.f. 2 (1936): 1–15; and Franz Unterkircher, ed., "Maximilian I 1459–1519 Ausstellung," *Bibleschriften* 23 (1959): 1–251, item 176; and W. C. McDonald and U. Goefel, *German Medieval Literary Pa-*

tronage from Charlemagne to Maximilian I (Amsterdam, 1975). The *Chronicon* of Hartmann Schedel (Nuremberg, 1493), folios 229–30, records similar portents associated with the plague of 1348. See Claude Jenkins "Dr. Hartmann Schedel and his book" in V. Ruffer and A. J. Taylor eds. *Medieval Studies Presented to Rose Graham* (Oxford, 1950): 98–137.

36. John Lydgate, *The Minor Poems of John Lydgate*, ed. H. N. MacCracken (London, 1934) EETS, o.s. 192, part 2, p. 702. See also Charles F. Mullett, "John Lydgate: A Mirror of Medieval Medicine," *Bulletin of the History of Medicine* 22 (1948): 403–15.

37. See John M. Riddle, "Pomum Ambrae: Amber and Ambergris in Plague Remedies," *Sudhoff's Archiv für Geschichte der Medizin und der Naturwissenschaften* 48 (1964): 111–22.

38. Mollaret and Brossollet, *La peste, source méconnue*, p. 20.

39. On Ketham, see Karl Sudhoff, ed. *The Fasciculus Medicinae of Johannes de Ketham*, trans. Charles Singer (Milan, 1924), pp. 42–45.

40. See Alfred Colville, "Écrits contemporaines sur la peste de 1348 à 1350" in *Histoire Littéraire de la France*, vol. 37 (Paris, 1938), pp. 349–51.

41. Olivier de la Haye, *Poème sur la grande peste de 1348*, ed. Georges Guigue (Lyon, 1888), xvii–xx.

42. See William C. McDonald, "Death in the Stars: Heinrich von Mügeln on the Black Plague," *Mediaevalia* 5 (1979): 89–109. McDonald, in my opinion, overestimates the originality of this work.

43. See the edition by E. Littré, "Opuscule relatif à la peste de 1348," *Bibliothèque de l'École des Chartes* 2 (1840–1841): 201–43. See also Christine Renardy, "Un témoin de la grande peste: Mâitre Simon de Couvin, chanoine de Saint-Jean l'évangéliste à Liège (1367)," *Revue belge de philologie et d'histoire* 52 (1974): 273–92. Renardy argues that Simon wished to ridicule the powerlessness of doctors and to show that the remedy for the plague comes from God alone if man is repentant. For a Middle Scots use of the work, see John B. Friedman, "Henryson's *Testament of Cresseid* and the *Judicio Solis in Conviviis Saturni* of Simon of Couvin," *Modern Philology* 82 (1985), to appear.

44. Thomas Brinton, *The Sermons of Thomas Brinton, Bishop of Rochester (1373–1389)*, ed. Mary Aquinas Devlin, vol. 2, sermon 70 (London, 1954), p. 323. See also the letters of Bishops la Zouche and Thorsby, quoted by A. Hamilton Thompson, "The Pestilences of the Fourteenth Century in the Diocese of York," *The Archaeological Journal* 71 (1914): 114.

45. See Lynn Thorndike, *Latin Treatises on Comets between 1238 and 1368* (Chicago, 1950), pp. 61–62, 176, 206, 224, 252–53 for texts connecting comets and plague. See generally Clarisse Doris Hellman, *The Comet of 1577: Its Place in the History of Astronomy* (New York, 1944) and Jean-Michel Massing, "A Sixteenth-Century Illustrated Treatise on Comets," *The Journal of the Warburg and Courtauld Institutes* 40 (1977): 318–22.

46. Priscilla Heath Barnum, ed., *Dives and Pauper* (London, 1976) EETS, o.s. 275, vol. 1, commandment 1, chap. 29, p. 147.

47. See Manilius, *Astronomica*, ed. and trans. G. P. Goold I.812–40, 872–97 (Cambridge, Mass. and London, 1977), pp. 71, 75.

48. See Hellman, *The Comet*, pp. 231–32, n. 139.

49. Henri of Ferrières, *Les Livres de Roy Modus et de la Royne Ratio*, ed. Gunnar Tilander, II.240 (Paris 1932), p. 200. A variety of other phenomena such

as floods, earthquake and civil unrest were associated with the plague. See generally M. E. Jeanselme, "Inondations, famines et tremblements de terre sont les avant-coureurs de la peste," *Proceedings of the Third International Congress of the History of Medicine, 1922* (Antwerp, 1923), pp. 37–41, and W. G. Cooke, "Fiery Drakes and Blazing Bearded Light," *English Studies* 61 (1980): 97–103. For particular examples, see Guillaume de Machaut, *Le jugement dou Roy de Navarre*, lines 143–80 in *Oeuvres de Guillaume de Machaut*, ed. Ernest Hoepffner (Paris, 1908-1921), vol. 1, pp. 142–43; Thomas Stubbs, *Lives of the Archbishops of York* in *Historians of the Church of York and its Archbishops*, ed. James Raine, 2 vols., Rolls Series, vol. 71 (reprint ed., Millwood, N.Y., 1964), 2:418; and Rossell Hope Robbins, ed., *Historical Poems of the XIVth and XVth Centuries* (New York, 1959), poem 20, lines 57–61, p. 59. For Machaut's catalogue, see David Lanoue, "History as Apocalypse: The 'Prologue' of Machaut's *Jugement dou Roy de Navarre*," *Philological Quarterly* 60 (1981): 1–12.

50. Raymond Chalmel de Viviers, *De peste*, book 1, chap. 1, p. 12.

51. Hans Folz, *Spruch von der Pest 1482*, ed. Ernest Martin (Strassburg, 1879), pp. 4–5.

52. Biraben, *Les hommes*, 1:409.

53. See generally, Biraben, *Les hommes*, 2:76–80; and, more recently, Pierre Rézeau ed. *Les prières aux saints en français à la fin du moyen âge* (Geneva, 1982).

54. Lydgate, *The Minor Poems,* part 1, EETS, o.s. vol. 107 (London, 1907). poem 57, p. 291.

55. Carleton Brown, ed., *Religious Lyrics of the XVth Century* (reprint ed., Oxford, 1962) no. 135, p. 206, lines 15–18.

56. This picture is discussed by Mollaret and Brossolet, *La peste, source méconnue*, pp. 61–62.

57. Gabriel de Mussis, *Ystoria de morbo*, p. 55. See also the poeticized description by the Welsh poet Jeuan Gethin in W. Rees, "The Black Death in England and Wales," *Proceedings of the Royal Society of Medicine* 16, History of Medicine section (1922-1923): 27–45.

58. For an excellent discussion of the main types of plague and their means of transmission, see Gottfried, *Epidemic Diseases*, pp. 58–62. See also Christos Bartsocas, "Two Fourteenth Century Greek Descriptions of the 'Black Death,'" *Journal of the History of Medicine* 21 (1966): 394–400.

59. A similar scene is depicted by the Master of Frankfort in a painting dated 1460 in the Wallraf-Richartz Museum in Cologne. See Albert S. Lyons and R. Joseph Petrucelli, *Medicine, An Illustrated History* (New York, 1978), p. 353, figure 540.

60. A representative group may be found in the horae of Keble College, Oxford. See MS. 1, sixteenth century, French, fol. 147ᵛ, suffrage and picture; MS. 6, fifteenth century, fol. 144ᵛ, suffrage and picture; MS. 40, fifteenth century, French, fol. 223ᵛ, suffrage and picture of martyrdom; MS. 41, French, atelier of Jean Colombe, late fifteenth century, fol. 179, suffrage and picture of martyrdom.

61. C. Wordsworth, ed., *Horae Eboracenses* Surtees Society, vol. 132, (Durham, 1920), p. 129.

62. On this painting, see Ilza Veith and Leo M. Zimmerman, "St. Sebastian and the Plague," *Bulletin of the Walters Art Gallery* 15 (1962), n.p.; Charles Sterling, "St. Sebastian Interceding for the Plague-Stricken," *Art Quarterly* 8

(1945): 216f. and "Josse Lieferinxe, peintre provençal," *La revue du Louvre* 14, no. 1 (1964): 1 and figure 14.

63. Mollaret and Brossollet, *La peste, source méconnue*, p. 79 and Paul Richer, *L'art et la médicine* (Paris, 1901), pp. 314–49.

64. See generally, Pedrizet, *La vierge*, p. 110; Marcel Fosseyeux, "Les Saints protecteurs contre la 'male' mort au moyen âge et à la renaissance," *Bulletin de la société française d'histoire de la médicine* 29 (1935): 339–49; Victor Kraehling, *Saint Sebastien dans l'art* (Paris, 1938); Harold Avery, "Plague Churches, Monuments and Memorials," *Proceedings of the Royal Society of Medicine* 59 (1966): 110–16; and Tristram, *Figures of Life and Death*, p. 177.

65. See Gelindo Ceroni, *San Rocco nella vita, nel culto, nell'arte* (Rome, 1927); A. Fliche, *Saint Roch* (Paris, 1930); Georges Guyonnet, "Saint Roch, le spécialiste des maladies contagieuses," *Histoire de la médicine* 1 (1959): 49–53; and Jean Segondy, "Saint Roch de Montpellier," *Monspeliensis Hippocrates* 23 (1964): 3–7.

66. Wordsworth, *Horae Eboracenses*, p. 131.

67. For an excellent overview of medieval confraternities, see Graham A. Runnals, "Mediaeval Trade Guilds and the *Miracles de Nostre Dame par personnages*," *Medium Aevum* 29 (1970): 257–76, especially 266–69, and Louis Du Broc de Segrange, *Les saints patrons des corporations et protecteurs* (Paris, n.d.) 1:61–64 and 2:156–59.

68. See K. L. Wood-Legh, "Some Aspects of the Histories of Chantries in the Later Middle Ages," *Transactions of the Royal Historical Society*, 4th ser. 23 (1946):47–60, and *Perpetual Chantries in Britain* (Cambridge, 1965).

69. Perhaps the most useful general study is George H. Cook, *Mediaeval Chantries and Chantry Chapels* (London, 1947).

70. This text is published by Heitz and Schreiber, *Pestblätter*, p. 25.

71. See, for example, the motto in a window in his honor at the church of St. Nizier, Troyes.

72. Published and discussed by Mollaret and Brossollet, *La peste, source méconnue*, p. 78.

73. See H. R. Storer, *Medicina in Nummis*, item 4458 (Boston, 1931), p. 601. See also item 6882, p. 915 for an amulet with a similar inscription. See further, Biraben, *Les hommes*, pp. 58–62.

74. See L. Pfeiffer and C. Ruland, *Pestilentia in Nummis* (Tübingen, 1882); Herman Wintz, "Munzen und Medaillen auf die Pest," *Ciba Zeitschrift* 30 (1936): 1022–26; and Bruno Kisch, "Plagues and Coins," *Ciba Symposium* 10 (Jan.–Feb. 1948): 807–10.

75. See John Harthan, *Books of Hours and their Owners* (London, 1977), pp. 152–53 and E. Millar, "Les Manuscrits peintures des Bibliothèques de Londres," *Bulletin de la société française de reproductions de manuscrits à peintures* (1920): 95–100.

76. De Smet, "Breve Chronicon," p. 16.

77. This miniature is discussed by J. W. S. Johnnson, "Documents iconographiques relatifs à la peste du XVe au XVIIIe siècle," *Bulletin de la société française d'histoire de la médicine* 10 (1911): 227–29 and figure 1.

78. Henri Mollaret and Jacqueline Brossollet, "La procession de Saint Gré-

goire et la peste à Rome en l'an 590," *Médicin de France* 199 (1969): 13–24.

79. See on this author Alfred Colville, "Gilles li Muisis, Abbé de Saint-Martin de Tornai, Chroniqueur et moraliste," *Histoire littéraire de la France*, vol. 37 (Paris, 1938), pp. 230–324. A miniature apparently modeled on that of li Muisis appears in a Russian chronicle of the plague of 1384 in the Leningrad Academy of Sciences Library. See Nikolai A. Bogoiavlenskii, *Drevnerrusskoe Vrachevanie* (Moscow, 1960), pl. 25, p. 109.

80. Gilles li Muisis, *Chronica Aegidii Le Muisis*, ed. J. J. de Smet in *Recueil des chroniques de Flandres*, 2:370, lines 293–95.

Fig. 1. Death, plague victim and burial, Boccaccio, *Decameron,* B.N. Ital. 482, fol. 6, ca. 1380. *Courtesy of* Bibliothèque Nationale.

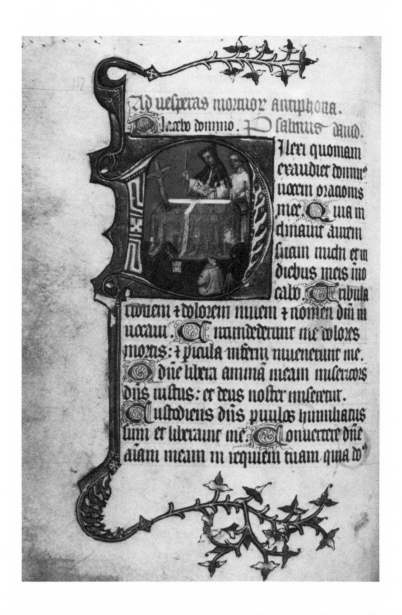

Fig. 2. Burial, horae, Keble College, Oxford MS. 15, fol. 68ᵛ, ca. 1375.
Courtesy of Master and Fellows, Keble College.

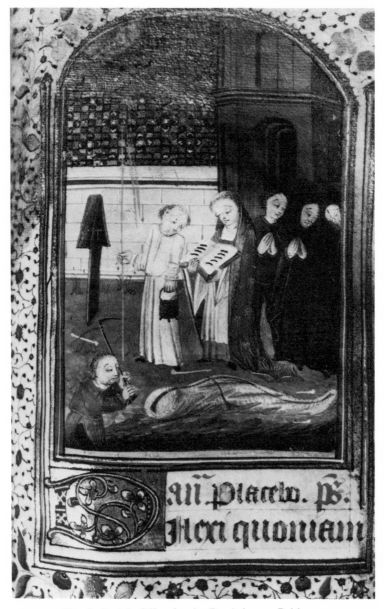

Fig. 3. Burial, Office for the Dead, horae, Poitiers,
Bibliothèque Municipale MS. 324, fol. 157ʳ, fifteenth century.

Fig. 4. Paul de Limbourg, burial of plague victims, *Très belles heures*,
New York, The Cloisters, fol. 74ʳ, ca. 1410.
Courtesy of The Cloisters.

Fig. 5. Jean Colombe, Horseman of the Apocalypse and corpses.
Nocturn from the Office for the Dead, *Très riches heures*, Chantilly,
Musée Condé, fol. 90ᵛ, fifteenth century. *Courtesy of* Musée Condé.

Fig. 6. Vengeful God with arrows, *pestblätt*, German, 15th century, after Paul Heitz and W. L. Schreiber, *Pestblätter des XV Jahrhunderts* (Strassburg, 1901), p. 3.

Fig. 7. Locusts, Jacob Mennel, *De Signis*, Vienna, Nationalbibliothek Palatine MS. 4417, fol. 11, 1503. *Courtesy of* Nationalbibliothek, Vienna.

Fig. 8. Pietro da Montagnana, physician and plague victim, John Ketham, *Fasciculus Medicinae* (Venice, 1495), sig. Diii[r].

Fig. 9. Comets, Jacob Mennel, *De Signis,* fol. 13.

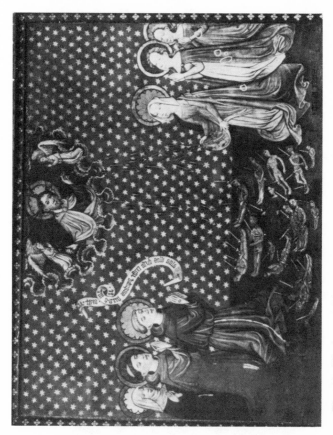

Fig. 10. Virgin and Plague victims, Altarpiece, church of the Carmelites, Göttingen, Hanover, Niedersächsische Landesgalerie, 1424. *Courtesy of Niedersächsische Landesgalerie.*

Fig. 12. *Der Peste*, Wallpainting, Swabia, Munich, Pinothek, 1510. *Courtesy of* Munich Pinothek.

Fig. 11. Saint Roch, horae, London BL MS Add. 18854 fol. 46ᵛ, ca. 1450. *Courtesy of* Trustees of the British Library.

Fig. 13. Josse Lieferinxe, Saint Sebastian interceding for victims of
the plague, Baltimore, Walters Art Gallery, 1497.
Courtesy of The Walters Art Gallery.

Fig. 14. Saint Sebastian with amulets, Soane Hours, London,
Sir John Soane Museum, fol. 112ᵛ ca. 1500.
Courtesy of Sir John Soane Museum.

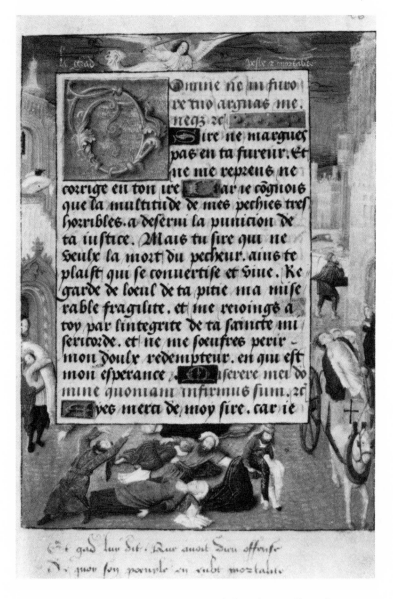

Fig. 15. Avenging angel and plague victims, horae, Copenhagen, Bib. Roy. Ny. Kon. Samling MS. 50, fol. 26, fifteenth century. *Courtesy of* Bib. Roy. Copenhagen.

Fig. 16. Paul de Limbourg, St. Gregory and Exterminating Angel, *Très riches heures*, fol. 72.

Fig. 17–18. Plague victims, horae, B.N. lat. 1393, fols. 110–110ᵛ, late fifteenth century. *Courtesy of* Bibliothèque Nationale.

Fig. 19. Burial of the dead, *Chronicle of Gilles li Muisis* 1349–1352, Brussels, Bibliothèque Royale MS. 13076–77, fol. 24ᵛ.
Courtesy of Bibliothèque Royale.

Fig. 20. Paul de Limbourg, burial scene, *Trés belles heures,* fol. 99.

Social Conscience and the Poets

Russell A. Peck

Preface

J OHN BALL SAINT MARY PRIEST, greeteth well all manner
of men, and biddeth them in name of the Trinitie, Father,
Sonne, & Holy Ghost, stand manlike together in truth,
& helpe truth, and truth shall helpe you.

> now raygneth pride in price,
> couetise is holden wise
> lechery without shame
> gluttonie without blame,
> enuye raygneth with reason,
> and sloath is taken in great season,
> God doe boote for nowe is time.
>   Amen.

Iohan schep, som-tyme seynte marie prest of ȝork, and now
of colchestre, Greteth wel Iohan nameles & Iohn þe mullere
and Iohon cartere, and biddeþ hem þei bee war of gyle in
borugh, and stondeth to-gidere in godes name, and biddeþ
Pers plouȝman / go to his werk and chastise wel hobbe þe
robbere; and takeþ wiþ ȝow Iohan Trewman and alle hijs
felawes and no mo, and loke schappe ȝow to on heued and
no mo.

> Iohan þe mullere haþ y-grounde smal, smal, smal.
> þe kynges sone of heuene schal paye for al.
> be war or þe be wo.
> Knoweþ ȝour freend fro ȝour foo.
> haueth y-now & seith hoo!
> and do wel and bettre and fleth synne,

and sekeþ pees and hold ȝow þer-inne.
and so biddiþ Iohan trewaman and alle his felawes.[1]

John Ball is often referred to as the spiritual leader of the Great
Revolt. His few surviving "letters" epitomize the spirit of much of
the subsequent reform literature as well. I do not mean to imply
direct literary influence or even to suggest that subsequent writers
thought in any way that they were writing in the spirit of John Ball.
In fact, most of the literary men I will deal with would have de-
tested the idea of any association with the renegade priest. But,
in truth, their writings share much in common with Ball's epistles.

Ball begins both his letters with a deliberately Pauline formula:
"John Ball Saint Mary Priest, greeteth well all manner of men ..."
etc. (Cf., "Paul, apostle of Christ, greets God's beloved saints ..."
etc., with which Paul commonly begins his epistles.) The formula
is especially pointed in that Ball, like St. Paul in several of his letters, addresses his friends from prison. The tone of Ball's epistles
is evangelistic, designed to link the audience directly to the spirit
of the early Christian church with its mythic simplicity. This is
the mood invoked in much of the later Wycliffite writings and also
in the *Piers Plowman* tradition (cf., Conscience's digression on "rect"
which Langland adds to Conscience's first speech in the C-text of
Piers [C.IV.317–419][2])—a mood of directness and openness which
might be thought of as a vernacular Truth. Ball's second epistle
provides one of the earliest literary allusions to Langland.[3] His
naming of "Pers plouman" as synonym for social conscience an-
ticipates what will become a dominant trope of social reform even
through the English renaissance.

Both letters exhort Ball's followers to stand together under "on
heued and no mo." This appeal for unity is likewise characteristic
of subsequent reform literature. The appeal of the Yorkshire Par-
tisans (1392) comes immediately to mind—"and yet will ilke-an hel
up other / and meynteyne him als his brother, / both in wrong &
right."[4] In a more subtle vein the idea appears in Gower's repeated
assertions that "Divisoun" is "moder of confusioun"[5] and in the mil-
itant cries of penitential literature to cling to the one Lord Jesus
in at-one-ment. The society of Piers' half acre is ruined when factions spring up like tares to despoil his economy, and the House
of Unity (B.XIX–XX) is desecrated by Antichrist's divisive hordes
—popes, priests, friars, merchants, and kings—all wanting private

temporalities and murdering to maintain them, rather than enjoy-
ing peace within the fold. But not only do Ball's letters appeal to
a spirit of Christian unity: they bid mankind to stand manlike together in truth. Two metaphors here reach deeply into the reform
tradition. The admonition to *stand* reminds the audience of bibli-
cal insistence on stouthearted decision — let there be no lukewarm
Laodicians among us; you are either for or against. Standing is
the manlike activity, what the serpent cannot do. Ball himself was
just so firm in his refusal to waver at his execution. So too the
priests at St. Albans and subsequent Wycliffite martyrs in the fifteenth century. Chaucer's Parson reminds his audience that all
penitential activity is, in effect, the taking of a stand, becoming
manlike again after the slovenliness of sin: "Stondeth upon the
weyes and seeth and axeth ... and walketh ... and ye shal finde
refresshynge for youre soules" (I.X.76–77.[6] His text is Jer. 6:16).
At the end of Gower's *Confessio Amantis*, after Genius has minutely
examined the lover's conscience, the lover rises from his cupidinous
thraldom on the forest floor to take his stand as John Gower, Christian citizen of England. The penitent Amans too has become manlike, at one with his estate.

A third point which Ball's letters share with the reform tradition
is the appeal to truth — stand manlike in truth. Ball's variation on
the popular formula from the Gospel of John (8:32) — "you shall
know the truth, and the truth shall make you free" — is stunningly
forceful in its application: "helpe truth, and truth shall helpe you."
The gospel passage provides a prominent motif in English literature of the last quarter of the fourteenth century. Gower expati-
ates upon the passage in the *Confessio Amantis*.[7] We find it again
in the refrain to Chaucer's poem "Truth: The Balade of Good Counsel," where "trouthe the shal delivere, it is no drede." We do not
normally think of Chaucer's well-tempered balade as social protest, but it in fact epitomizes revolutionary thought as late fourteenth-century Christians perceived it: "Reule wel thiself, that other
folk canst rede"; "Daunte thiself, that dauntest otheres dede"; "Hold
the hye wey, and lat thy gost the lede" ("Truth," lines 6, 13, 20).[8]
Reform must start with individuals who, through their personal
search for truth, become models for others. Even in Ball's letters,
where the message is explicitly directed toward the social conscience
of his audience, the appeal is to individual consciences in their search
for truth.[9] To the "hold the hye wey" advice he would add, "and

be alert." But whether in Chaucer, Langland, Gower, *Richard the Redeless*, or *Mum and the Sothsegger*, the advice to seek truth and liberation guided by one's "gost" appears again and again. The greatest exploration of the idea that man's individual deliverance lies in truth occurs in the intricate search for St. Truth in *Piers Plowman*, though the expansions upon the notion in *Piers Plowman's Crede* and *Mum and the Sothsegger* are in their own ways impressive.

One final point that I would make about the Ball epistles is to note their sense of urgency—"for now is time." Though penitential literature, advice-to-kings literature, satires against evil counsellors, and Wycliffite attacks on abuses within the church may seem to us long-winded and often formless, such literature is nonetheless characterized by a fierce restlessness and a sense of the immediacy of time's demands. Apocalyptic metaphors frequently crop up. The appeal is to *doing*—doing well now—even though the narrator, like Will in *Piers*, may be utterly uncertain of what it is that doing well or better entails. Nevertheless, he seems compelled, driven to doing something—to "do wel and bettre" now.

Though some have argued that the Peasant's Revolt in itself accomplished nothing, it is my contention that in the three decades following the "hurling time"[10] we see truly basic changes in the medieval psyche occurring, which irrevocably affect the English church, the monarchy, and most important of all, the individual's perception of himself. My discussion concentrates on the aftermath of 1381 and is divided into two sections. First I discuss relationships between Wycliffite and penitential literature and their bearing on political and ecclesiastical reform and, more importantly, upon perceptions of individual conscience. Then I examine vernacular literature of the 1390s and the first decade of the fifteenth century to illustrate a blending of Langland and Chaucer traditions to which sixteenth-, eighteenth-, and nineteenth-century reform movements looked for inspiration and propaganda.

I.

In his 1976 Medieval Academy address on "Dissent in Middle English Literature: The Spirit of (Thirteen) Seventy-six," Rossell Hope Robbins makes two points which I wish to reemphasize at the outset of my argument. After dismissing the sporadic but ubiquitous abuses-of-the-age verses as little more than traditional formulas of complaint ("What was amiss in 1300 was still amiss in 1500"[11] — the sentiments, even the rhymes, are the same), Robbins observes: "The most dangerous and far-reaching manifestations of dissent are to be found, not so much in the tags current in the Peasant's Revolt, but in the works of pro-Establishment writers. The best examples come in the *unconscious* formulations by men like Langland and Wyclif, both fundamentally conservative, of basically dissident positions, that only later move from philosophical criticism and genteel reform to open rebellion. It took the medieval 'establishment,' which had let Wyclif die in peace, some thirty years to realize that his doctrines were being used for subversion and ultimately to exhume and burn his remains."[12] Though the degree of "unconsciousness" which Robbins implies needs qualification, let me move to the second point upon which I wish to build, a point more intricate, though corollary to the first.

Robbins emphasizes the inseparability of religious and political issues in fourteenth-century Europe. "Wyclif," he argues, "brought together a body of reformist views previously expressed only separately, and by coalescing them revealed their latent radicalism" — views such as Grosseteste's challenging of papal claims, his emphasis on preaching, and his appeal to the Bible as the primary authority; Ockham's attack on papal views on temporalities, indeed, upon the very principles upon which papal authority rested; and Fitzhugh's opposition to friars and the doctrine of dominion.[13] Although Wyclif's reasoning led him to question the necessity of the sacraments, the mediative power of the priesthood, and papal authority, the immediate effect of his teaching was less theological than political. Wyclif received support from many noblemen and churchmen, including renegade friars, in his attacks on ecclesiastical hierarchy, temporalities, indulgences, simony, and tithing. He also received enthusiastic responses from people in all three estates for his preaching and writing in the vernacular and his insistence on every individual's responsibility in establishing "a lyne streght unto heven."[14] "Few realized," Robbins points out, "the political implications of his condemnation of purely religious practices. Philosophically, as it turned out, Wyclif was more dangerous to the Establishment than John Ball. By abolishing the doctrinal distinction between clergy and laity, Wyclif obliterated one of the Three Estates on which, according to traditional theory, not only the well-being but the very existence of a nation rested.[15]

The full impact of the Wycliffite movement on late fourteenth-century English literature and society is only beginning to be appreciated. Some have denigrated Wyclif's importance by demonstrating that many of the English writings once attributed to him he did not write. But if anything, that line of observation underscores rather than diminishes his role as mentor and spokesman. Of the movement itself we have little hard evidence. K. B. McFarlane notes that once the movement is forced underground it becomes almost impossible to trace.[16] We only know that it spread rapidly in the 1380s. Although it was concerned primarily with church reform, by the 1390s some issues had spread to the political arena and were given lively debate in Parliament. During the first decades after Wyclif's death in 1382, Wycliffite preaching—with its emphasis on scripture, personal salvation, and its attack on specific ecclesiastical abuses—apparently addressed to some extent the restlessness, frustration, and spiritual needs of common people throughout England. Moreover, it appealed to merchants, guildsmen, and the intelligent gentry as well.

The matter is complicated by the fact that Wyclif himself is part of a larger penitential movement which, being directed toward individual conscience, appears to be politically conservative (if it can be said to be political at all), but which ultimately ends up being radically apolitical—a matter between the soul and God, which may be as threatening to Caesar and his officers as more aggressively designed schemes of social dissent. Occasionally one encounters in historical records evidence of hard-core Wycliffite activity, like the publishing of the Twelve Lollard Conclusions on the door of St. Paul's in 1395, but usually the activity is scarcely discernible from more orthodox appeals to repent of the sins of the world. Perhaps the distinguishing feature of the penitential movement in the later fourteenth century, besides the proliferation of penitential handbooks in the vernacular, is the strong emphasis on the individual, his conscience, and personal choice.

The idea that each man is his own priest is not exclusive with Wyclif; rather, it is a basic tenet of early Christianity which is rediscovered—or, rather, reemphasized—as preachers and laymen start talking about a simpler, more evangelical Christianity like that depicted in Acts and St. Paul's epistles, scenes like that in Chaucer's *Second Nun's Tale*, where small groups gather together in the evening for prayer and meditation, despite political censor-

ship. The penitential movement is marked by an increase in vernacular meditations, confessions written in English, and homiletic
exercises for and even by lay folk: works like Clanvowe's *The Two
Ways* and the penitential wills of John Cheyne, Lewis Clifford, and
Thomas Latimer, as well as meditational material like the Westmidland prose psalter, the meditations, epistles and psalter of the
hermit Richard Rolle whom Wycliffite writers interpolated (the hermit too disliked liturgical pomp and emphasized Bible study), and,
of course, the later English mystics.

There is little information available whereby we may trace the
penitential movement at court. It seems to have begun early in the
century and doubtless was stimulated by the crises of the Black
Death. Blanche, duchess of Lancaster, is reputed to have been a
deeply religious woman.[17] One tradition holds that she encouraged
the writing of vernacular literature and that Chaucer translated
the *ABC* for her personal meditation.[18] Anne of Bohemia, Richard's queen, is also reputed to have been devout, an advocate of
vernacular meditation, and of peace policies with France.[19] It is
conceivable that the influence of great women such as these may
have had something to do with the favor Wyclif and reform-minded
preachers found with John of Gaunt, Richard, and the various
serious-minded knights and civil servants who were employed by
the royal family — men like John Clanvowe, Lewis Clifford, William Nevill, and Richard Sturry (the so-called Lollard Knights).[20]

That this kind of religious activity was conducted in English is
of crucial importance. It made possible for all people a participatory religion with emphasis on doing — albeit a metaphysical doing — which addressed itself directly to "the vale of restless mind."[21]
That the use of the vernacular was in itself a major act of rebellion
against long established tradition has been stressed by McFarlane
and Robbins, and, in fact, went not unnoticed in the fourteenth
century as objections were raised against the translating of Holy
Writ into English, whereby subjects might make decisions for themselves and thus rebel against sovereignty.[22] Many a clergyman
must have been ill at ease when "Boke" with his "two brode eyen"
(*Piers Plowman* B.XVIII.228–29) fell into the hands of the laity. But
others were devoting their lives and consciences to just such practices, confident that every man should be trained to make informed
and reasonable assessments of his own culpability, guided by his
conscience and the Bible.[23]

Chaucer's Parson provides a familiar example of penitential issues as he preaches simply and directly from Scripture, with exempla from the writings of the learned saints. He addresses his audience as individuals, desiring to show each the nature and value of penance. He translates and explicates his texts phrase by phrase so that the seeker of penitential satisfaction may discover for himself this "ful noble wey" to God. He is more a guide than a mediator, a guide to questions the soul must put to itself if it is to find hope. The Parson is accused by other pilgrims of being a Lollard when he is first called on to speak. There is little in his sermon which one would normally associate with Lollard heresies. By the same token, there is little in the sermon that a Wycliffite minister might object to. And there is much, especially in method and intention, which the fundamentalist would applaud: the emphasis on grace and personal salvation; the celebration of the burning love of God which kindles desire for penance; the criticism of superfluity of dress; the detestation of war; the classification of abortion, birth control, and child abandonment as forms of manslaughter (cf. conclusions eleven and twelve in the Lollard manifesto of 1395 which abhor these last sins in particular); the stipulation that the priest be clean of sin himself if he is to minister; and the stressing of personal intention and honesty in pursuit of spiritual renewal.[24] To Harry Bailly and the Shipman, who complains against the Parson's moralizing on clean speech, any hint of reform smells of Lollardy (II [B]. 1172–83). But in truth, the term Lollard is thrown about so loosely in the two decades after Wyclif that it is virtually useless as anything other than a term of scorn. Sometimes it is used to indicate laziness; sometimes to indicate heresy or doctrinal disagreement; sometimes as an indication of bad seed—cockle in clean corn [cf. *lolia:* tares]. Certainly it does not consistently imply a specific set of doctrines which were held by a definable group of dissidents. The Wycliffite author of *Piers Plowman's Crede* uses it as a label to deride friars![25]

In view of the vernacular penitential tradition of the later fourteenth century, Chaucer's unabashedly autobiographical Retraction is a fit conclusion to the *Canterbury Tales*. A generation earlier one might have expected a different kind of conclusion, perhaps the more common formula of going to mass to see the host which priests show everyday. But the Retraction, with its prayer for forgiveness and mercy despite "giltes" and "worldly vanities," and its open declaration of desire for penitence, confession, and satisfaction in hope of salvation "at the day of doom," is identical in tone to the written "conclusions" to the real lives of several of Chaucer's "Lollard" friends, such as Clanvowe's *The Two Ways*, a homily Clanvowe seems to have written in his last year while he was on pilgrimage to the Holy Land, and the so-called Lollard wills of John and Edward Cheyne, Thomas Latimer, and Lewis Clifford, which McFarlane discusses.[26]

The point of my excursion into details of this kind is not to argue that Clanvowe or Chaucer were Wycliffians or incipient Lollards, but rather to emphasize the tenor of the penitential movement in which so many prominent people were to some considerable extent involved. It is a movement which placed heavy personal responsibility upon the individual, even if he be a layman. It is a movement which develops subtle new meanings for conscience. The term *conscience* comes to English from Late Latin through Old French, the earliest instances appearing in the thirteenth century but with a proliferation of usages in the last quarter of the fourteenth century as *conscience* displaces the native word *inwit*. In its earlier meaning conscience is the functional capacity of a rational man's soul to convey consciousness of right and wrong. According to the *OED* the word originally had no plural in English, conscience being viewed rather as a common property, a joint-knowledge. However, "it came gradually to be thought of as an individual entity, a member or organ of the mental system, of which each man possessed *one*, and thus it took *a* and plural. So *my conscience* and *your conscience*, was understood to mean no longer our respective shares or amounts of the common quality of conscience, but to be two distinct individual consciences, mine and yours."[27] The first recorded instance of the plural form in English is in the Wyclif Bible (2 Cor. 5:11). (Actually the plural form is found in the Vulgate.) In fact, many of the first English uses of the various shades of meaning of the word which the *OED* and the *Middle English Dictionary* cite come from the Wyclif Bible, especially from the Pauline epistles. Paul accounts for twenty-six of the thirty-three instances of the term in the Vulgate. Paul variously uses *conscientia* to mean inward knowledge, consciousness, mental recognition, sense of right and wrong, remorseful accusation, and "the testimony and secret judgment of the soul which gives its approbation to actions that it thinks good."[28] It is understandable that Paul's usage of the term would become basic material in penitential literature because he is viewed by the medieval church as the archetypal pilgrim.[29]

The term conscience frequently appears in Chaucer, especially in works like *Melibee,* the *Friar's Tale,* the *Second Nun's Tale,* the *Parson's Tale* and *Boece,* which are concerned with the intricacies of moral choice. Gower uses it to define a prelate's sense of obligation to Holy Church (*Confessio Amantis,* Prologue 297), to define an area in the soul for the plotting of evil (II.2844), to define one's faculty for making moral choices (III.11 and IV.792), to indicate inner feelings (III.1504), and as a receptacle for divine inspiration (VI.1906). Gower does not personify conscience in the *Confessio,* since the guiding decisions of the sort that conscience might make to help Amans are made by Genius, who functions as roughly the equivalent to conscience. We should note, however, that apart from Amans himself Genius is the principal character in the poem.

It is *Piers Plowman,* of course, that develops concepts of conscience most elaborately. Conscience appears in three separate sequences as a personified character. In the first sequence the Visio-king calls his "knyʒte Conscience" from beyond the sea to help him judge the worth of Lady Meed (B.III.109ff.). Apart from the immediate satiric point directed against England's war policy, in which it would seem that England's conscience has been abroad during the French wars, Langland works within the traditional scholastic view that the king (Intellect) should be guided by two counsellors, Conscience and Reason. In *De Officio Regis,* Wyclif, following the *Secreta Secretorum,* argues that real kings should be guided by Reason and Truth, then law, which may in some situations be overruled. The ruling king must first govern himself conscientiously according to divine law if he is to provide the supporting walls for his kingdom.[30] In Langland, the King's Conscience requests Reason's advice on whether he should kiss Meed. Conscience is the guardian of common profit and personal integrity — the boundaries — within the state. His conscientiousness protects the kingdom from False (or perhaps I should say, tries to protect). As we shall see, Langland shifts the emphasis somewhat from the B- to the C-text, giving the king even greater autonomy, perhaps in accord with Wyclif's absolutist views of monarchy. But the main point here is that Langland initially works within a traditional scholastic framework — one shared emphatically by Wyclif — in which the king, guided by Conscience and Reason, should be able to govern justly and in-dependently of such contingencies as Lady Meed and her suitors.

The second appearance of Conscience occurs after the first dream sequence in the *Vita* in which Will has undertaken an inward journey guided by Thought, Wit and Inwit, Dame Study (Wit's wife), Clergye and his wife Scripture, Kynde, and Imaginatif. When Will sleeps again, after contemplating Imaginatif's instruction, Conscience comforts him and guides him to meet Patience in the court of Clergye, then on to Haukyn (*activa vita*), and finally to Anima. That is, Conscience is Will's guiding companion in his journey toward his discovery of his soul. Conscience here is a more subtle figure than the Conscience of the Visio-king. He functions as a combination of natural and learned abilities in the earlier passus which better enable Will to control his temper and make right choices. Willi Erzgräber has shown how Langland's Conscience combines two scholastic terms — *conscientia* (shared knowledge) and *synderesis* (higher power of discernment) — whereby he enjoys a natural power to stir the soul toward good.[31] In this section of the *Vita*, Conscience seems to be truly a personal guide.

The final encounter with Conscience occurs after Will's vision of the Passion (B.XIX–XX). This time Conscience serves Will both as a personal guide and a social phenomenon, a social conscience, which help Will to understand degenerative processes within Christian history. After explaining to Will the various names of Jesus, Conscience is crowned by Grace as a king with Craft as his steward, Piers as his reeve, and with oxen, seed, and house to establish and maintain a Christian community. But his role as social Conscience is marked by one disaster after another. In fact, all his defensive schemes seem doomed to fail. He can produce church hierarchies to help administer the House of Unity, build a moat around it to protect it from Antichrist's hundreds, introduce penitential movements during plagues, and even call friars in an effort to counteract the spread of evil. But the world is such that whatever Conscience produces is immediately corrupted — even the papacy proclaims itself a worldly power, makes war, slays men whom it should save, and "pileth holykirke" (B.XIX.407–55). The final blow comes when the soon-corrupted friars pervert the very penitential process itself by adopting the ailing Contrition into "oure fraternyte for a litel sylver" so that Contrition "clene" forgets to weep and cry (B.XX.365–67). With that, Conscience (i.e., personal conscience) sets out again as a pilgrim to walk wide in the world in search of Piers Plowman. So the poem concludes. As social conscience fails, the only hope seems to lie with personal conscience, and that quite alone in a desert.

Langland is not alone among fourteenth-century men of letters, however, in holding this disenchanted view that only individuals, not societies, can be redeemed. *Sir Gawain and the Green Knight* ends with a disturbing tension between what personal conscience has discovered about itself and what society's conscience is able to accept and live with. In the literature that takes off from *Piers Plowman* it is the frustrated conclusion to that poem which writers respond to most. *Piers Plowman's Creed*, as we shall see, is built upon the dilemma of a seeker who finds only falseness in the institutions surrounding him; the pattern is the same in *Mum and the Sothsegger*. In both it is the personal conscience of the narrator along with a passion for truth which enables him to confirm his belief, despite what society tells him.

But let me end this discussion of conscience on a more positive note. In the individual conscience there is much to hope for. Consider the first lyric by the Digby 102 poet, entitled "Love God and drede," a poem written, according to J. Kail, about 1400.[32] Like other poems in the Digby manuscript, "Love God and drede" responds to several political issues that had recently been debated in Parliament: threats of tyranny, secret hatred between factions, and self interest. The poet admonishes quarreling parties to make peace, inveighs against judges taking bribes and selling the laws, and blames those who condemn a man without hearing his apology. But the main thrust of the poem is not to a corrupt society at large but to individual consciences. Its refrain "knowe thyself, love God, and drede" hammers the point home repeatedly. (The poet uses variation on the refrain in several of his poems: e.g., "Man know thyself and learn how to die" [VII] and "Know thyself and thy God" [XXII].) Several of the ideas in the poem appear to derive from Chaucer's moral balades. The refrain "know thyself, love God and drede" and such admonitions as "Drede god and knowe thyself" (line 9), or "And lawe be kept, no folk nyl ryse" (line 63), and "Govern thy puple in unyte" (line 21) hearken back to Chaucer's *Lak of Stedfastness*, with its advice to the Prince: "Dred God, do law, love trouthe and worthinesse / And wed thy folk agayn to stedfastnesse" (lines 27–28). Similarly, Chaucer's line "for hord hath hate" ("Truth," line 13) seems to lie behind "old horded hate maketh wrathe to rise" (line 165). Exemplified throughout the poem is Chaucer's sentiment, "Reule wel thyself, that other folk canst rede," which I discussed earlier in connection with John Ball (cf., "Drede god, and knowe thyselue, / That ouer puple hast gouernaunce" [lines 9–10]). But even more emphatically than Chaucer, the Digby poet stresses individual responsibility and the ability of conscience to guide man — "eche man," as he repeatedly puts it (cf., lines 1, 17, 25, 97, 141):

> Mannes conscience wil hym telle,
>> Riche and pore, fool and wyse,
> Whether he be worthi heuene or helle
>> To resceyue, after his seruyce.
> Eche man auyse him, that is wys,
>> Pore, and prynce styf on stede,
> Or vyces ouer vertues rys.
>> Man, knowe thy self, loue god, and drede.
>> (lines 137–44)

Despite the failures of institutions to provide sound moral guidance, man has his conscience, that inner voice that "wil hym telle."

But let me return to Wyclif, whose relationship with the penitential movement and the growth of individual consciousness was not the only area in which he helped to provoke change in medieval consciousness. Wyclif and his followers were protected by men associated with the court and royal policy. It was not simply Wyclif's attack on the papacy and temporalities that made him attractive to the monarchy. Principally, it was his defense of regal authority — the allowing of the king, in cases of need, privileges beyond the law and Parliament as well as beyond ecclesiastical dominion. The idea is based upon the familiar analogy between the state and man. In *De Officio Regis* (1378) Wyclif argues that the king "in times of his realm's or his own necessity may take the temporal possessions both of the laity and of the clergy. For thus does the heart in its necessity to draw heat and moisture from every possible member."[33] In the two decades following Wyclif's death opponents warned that such theories not only undermined the church but the foundation of the nobility as well.[34] But the monarchy looked upon Wyclif not as a threat but rather as an ally — even an ally against the nobles as well as the church. His attack upon the sacraments was less important than his firm monarchist support. Richard

Kaeuper has suggested that Wycliffite attacks on temporalities
served the monarchy in the manner of an intimidating police dog
which could be brought out barking in fiscal emergencies whenever
the monarchy needed more revenues from the clergy, who in the
presence of such threatening noises would become more docile and
generous than was its wont. Actually, the police-dog precedent precedes Richard's reign and Wyclif's propaganda. Ockhamite friars
advised Parliament during an invasion scare in 1371 that all possessions, including those of the clergy, should be held common and
at the king's disposal in all cases of necessity.[35] McKisack observes
that Wyclif was in attendance at that session as a spectator newly
in the employ of the crown[36] — an example, perhaps, of Edward's
teaching a young dog old tricks. Several times in the reigns of
Richard II and Henry IV the same tactic was used as the question
of whether possessioners should be relieved of their benefices was
opportunely reintroduced.

The tactic was more successful when used against the church
than against the nobles and commons, however. The struggle between the king and the nobility remained a prominent issue throughout the fourteenth century.[37] But despite the fact that Richard
failed in his attempt to be independent of lordly constraints he was
surely aware of what he was doing, and he knew that his form of
political revolution was a dangerous game. But it was one he expected to win. Perhaps his idea of royal autonomy went back to
the Peasant's Revolt itself, his most glorious day, when he outfaced
the rebel mob while noblemen like his half brother the earl of Kent
and Sir John Holland abandoned him to save their own skins by
scrambling to safety. It was commoners like Mayor Walworth, John
Philipot, and Nicholas Brembre who stood by him, struck down
Wat Tyler, and managed to collect a force from within London
as Richard stood alone as "leader" of the rebels, albeit utterly in
their hands. It is understandable that in years to come this king
would look for counsellors among talented men whom he could trust,
even though they were from the dirt, rather than honoring treach-
erous feudal alignments. Nor was he likely to forget or forgive in-
fringements against his favorites when the Lords Appellant and
their "Merciless Parliament" deprived him of advisors like Simon
Burley and his long valued friend Nicholas Brembre. McFarlane
is surely correct in characterizing as patient, brooding, and utterly
calculated Richard's nearly successful attempt to destroy all five

of the Appellants over the next decade.[38] The incipient revolution of political theory upon which he embarked was the centralization of authority more strongly under the monarchy. It was not until the Tudors that that goal was accomplished. But Richard had the idea. Moreover, the mob had come to him.

In her recent study, *The Theme of Government in Piers Plowman*, Anna Baldwin demonstrates with some thoroughness the large extent to which Langland's political views correspond with Wyclif's, especially in the revisions of the C-text and in those sections in the *Visio* where the king and the rest of England compete for Lady Meed.[39] We do not normally think of *Piers* in the Mirror-for-Princes tradition, but if Baldwin is right (and I think she is) *Piers* enjoys an influential place there. Langland's poem is a primary source for subsequent advisory literature such as *Richard the Redeless*, *Mum and the Sothsegger*, *The Crowned King*, and the Digby 102 poems. Not all treat monarchial authority in the same way, however. The later poets usually advise Henry against absolutist tendencies.

But, according to Wyclif, the king by natural law can override a corrupted common law, providing he be guided by reason and conscience. In giving the king Reason and Conscience as his chief advisors in the *Visio* section of *Piers*, "Langland," Baldwin suggests, "is setting the scene for the king's direct judgment according to the principles of equity."[40] This may explain why Langland removed from the C-text Prologue all passages which suggested that the king should rule according to law or Parliament. "When a king judged through his prerogative courts he acted as an absolute monarch. Indeed, contemporary Parliaments treated the development of equity as a most suspicious growth of the king's political power."[41] Langland's satire examines Meed's corrupting marriages, especially in local governments where sheriffs, justices of the peace, sisors, and jurors are owned by great men and thus represent a serious threat to the king's government. Meed devours the king's wealth; when it becomes evident that the king has not gained what was his due, rather than correct the abuses, Meed simply advocates that the king wring more from his poor commons. The passages go back to the A-text of *Piers*. They reflect the very situations the peasants revolted against in 1381. As Baldwin points out, "Retinues bought through Meed can only ... stifle legal and administrative impartiality in the provinces, in the central courts, and in the boroughs. If the king tries to create a court party in the same way, he can say farewell to justice in peace or war."[42]

Langland develops the point in the contest between Peace and Wrong (C.IV). The abused Peace demonstrates "how the country has been given over to crime and oppression by the king's failure to control the power of his nobles, and by his own compromises with Meed."[43] The king acts absolutely as he rejects Wrong's compromise, realizing that to allow him to buy his way out only further harms the poor and peaceable men whom Wrong oppresses. The king insists on justice, appealing to the equity of Conscience and Reason rather than law or Parliament.

With the possible exception of Gower, most of the poets who deal with political issues in the latter part of the century would agree, in essence, with the position Langland outlines in the *Visio*. The key to validating the royalist argument lies in the extent to which the king acts according to good conscience and reason. If the king follows Meed's counsel, his absolutism is likely to prove abortive. This is precisely the point which *Richard the Redeless* attacks when the poet ridicules the fashions of Richard's court and the haughty oppression of common people by men in the king's livery. Rather than rule with Conscience and Reason, Richard has used Meed to sustain his own private retinue which struts about the realm with slit sleeves and elbows that must reach to the heel else the proud courtier be "wroth as the wynde and warie hem that it made" (III.153).[44] When an honorable old courtier appears in the court in his "sclavin," he is mocked and driven out with a pick axe by the porter while the "sleves that slode uppon the erthe" cry out "slay him," and "berdless burnes" bay after him and mock "his slaveyn ... of the olde schappe" (III.235-37). We are told that the old man's name is Witt. The poet wonders how a king who began with such advantages—a crown adorned with gems and virtues, the richest of any in Christendom—could so foolishly lose it all, not only spoiling the broth, but even casting the crock into the ashes. But the loss is inevitable when Witt is driven from the court. Without well-intended wit, conscience becomes evil-conscience.

It is remarkable how frequently questions of right-governance come up in late fourteenth-century English literature, even before Richard's overthrow. Chaucer's attitude is succinctly mirrored in the envoy to *Lak of Stedfastnesse* where the poet addresses the conscience of the king: "O Prince, desyre to be honourable, / Cherish thy folk and hate extorcioun! / Suffre nothing that may be reprevable / To thyn estat don in thy regioun" (lines 22–25). Chaucer's view here is comparable to the absolutist attitude in the *Tale of Melibee*, where Prudence (i.e., right reason)[45] works with Melibee's conscience until he is persuaded to prefer mercy to vengeance. It is evident that Melibee could have retaliated against his enemies, despite Prudence, at any time he chose, though the likelihood of success had he done so would have been dim. As ruler, Melibee enjoys a kind of absoluteness which he could abuse, if Reason and Conscience failed to convince him otherwise. In Gower the theme of right rule and the prerogatives of office are also prominent. Like Langland, Gower insists that the king must be guided by Reason and Conscience. But he is less willing to allow the king an absolutist position, adhering more closely to Bracton's position which limits the monarch's power, placing him explicitly beneath the law.[46] Although Gower began the *Confessio* as a poem "for king Richardes sake," by 1392 he seems to have lost hope in Richard's cause. Only insofar as "king" is metaphor for the governance of the soul does Gower allow for an absolute sovereignty. And even here the "king" is more an administrator under divine, natural, and positive laws than an absolutist.

II.

Thus far I hope to have established three points: 1) an intimacy between Wycliffite reform and a larger penitential movement which focuses attention on the vernacular and the individual soul's conscience in a direct relationship with God; 2) an attack on the temporal features of the established church, especially the worldliness of the papacy; 3) the prominence of Wycliffite ideas pertaining to monarchy which provoke extensive discussion of the limits of the royal office. I have worked from the assumption that all three areas are loosely connected with the Peasant's Revolt insofar as they share concerns to which the revolt called attention. Moreover, I have attempted to show some influence of these concerns upon proestablishment writers of the 1380s, especially Langland, Chaucer, and Gower.

I now wish to turn attention to writers of the mid-1390s and the following decade who bring Langland, Chaucer, and Gower together to establish a legacy of literary protest to which later generations look back for inspiration in the completing of the changes and reforms which began in the 1380s. I will deal mainly with three Wycliffite works — *Piers Plowman's Crede*, *The Plowman's Tale*, and *Jack Upland*, the latter two of which were attributed to Chaucer by Reformation propagandists. All three are stinging attacks on ecclesiastical corruption, and especially upon the friars. Of the three, *Piers Plowman's Crede* is the most sophisticated and skillfully written. The poet, writing about 1394,[47] has complete mastery of Langland's alliterative line and shares with the earlier poet an eye for precise realistic details which he manipulates with wit and an epigrammatic forcefulness as he strikes brilliantly at confraternal affluence. So exact is he in his accounts of the physical layout of Franciscan and Dominican convents that one is inclined to agree with Wright that he must have been a renegade friar.[48] At the outset of the poem the narrator announces that he knows his Pater noster and Ave marie, but not his Creed. Perturbed by fear of what penance this deficiency might require, he sets out to find some "werldly wi3t" (line 17)[49] who might teach him what to believe. First he goes to the Grayfriars, suggesting that if they cannot help him the Carmelites might. The Franciscan responds by attacking the promiscuity and gluttony of the Carmelites — "Maries men" who "lieþ on our Ladie many a longe tale" (lines 48–49). Only the Grayfriars can show the "pure Apostelles life" (line 104), since they so value poverty and piety. The friar immediately contradicts himself, however, as he announces the new church they are building which needs windows: give money and you shall be placed near St. Francis himself in the west window, near the middle, where your name shall be nobly written and "y-rade þer for euer" (line 129). That is not the kind of immortality the narrator had expected, however, and though the minorite reassures him that he need not bother about the Creed if the friars "asoilen" him (line 132), he leaves, disappointed at the friar's backbiting, consoling himself like a good Wycliffite with Holy Scripture (Matt. 7:1–4, 20; Luke 12:15).

He next tries the Dominicans. Immediately he is struck by the splendor of the great convent with its painted pillars "queynteli i-coruen wiþ curiouse knottes" (line 161), well-wrought windows bearing coats of arms of merchants (more than "twenty and two twyes y-noumbred" — line 178), handsome walls with privy posterns, orchards and arbors, a tabernacle so well-decorated that it would cost more than the "pris of a plou3land ... To aparaile þat pyler" (lines

169–70), tombs for knights and lovely ladies whose likenesses are carved in alabaster and marble to make them look like saints: ten years of taxes "trewly y-gadered" could not pay for half (line 189). Upon entering the cloister the narrator stands agape at the extravagance of leadwork and paved walkways; the chapter house is grand "as a Parlement-hous" (line 202), the refectory fit "for an hyʒe kinge" (line 210) and glassed as if it were a church. The chambers have chimneys, the "dortour y-diʒte wiþ dores ful stronge" (line 211), while adjacent houses are fit "to herberwe þe queene" (line 215). "And ʒet þise bilderes wilne beggen a baggful of wheate / Of a pure pore man þat maie oneþe paie / Half his rente in a ʒer and half ben behynde" (lines 216–18). In the refectory the narrator meets a great fat friar, whose flesh wags "as a quyk mire" (line 226), seated like a tun upon a bench, "biclypped" with his "double worsted" cope (line 228). The friar boasts about the antiquity of his order — "oure foundement was first of þe oþere" (line 250) — and claims Dominican learnedness makes them worthy to become popes. The narrator, in disgust, leaves, again citing to himself passages from the Gospels (Matt. 20:26 and Luke 10:18), which remind him that Christ preached a doctrine of service and humility rather than lazy pride. The juxtaposition of rich and poor is ever present in his consciousness.

Next he meets an Augustinian friar, who is no help with Creed either, though he too can attack other friars. The narrator is "assoiled" once more, providing he "helpe us hertiliche" to "amendeth oure hous in money oþer elles" (lines 319–21), though he knows it is an empty gesture — "Here Crede is coueyteise" (line 337). On the road he meets two Carmelites who vigorously attack the Dominicans for their pride and arrogance; it is the Carmelites who are most ancient, descended from Elijah. They too ask for money for their building and will "assoile" him without his having to learn the Creed, except that they do not have time to linger, for one must hasten to collect £10 from a "houswife" and the other to "henten ʒif y mighte / An Anuell for myn owen use" (lines 413–14). Discouraged at the falsity of the friars, the narrator wanders until he meets "a sely man" who hangs "opon þe plow" (line 421). The plowman is poorly clothed, up to his ankles in mud, and accompanied by an ill-clad wife whose bare feet are bleeding as she shivers with her two hungry and crying children. The plowman, named Piers, asks why the narrator is so unhappy, thus learning of his disap-

pointing quest for instruction. Piers attacks all friars — "þei ben wilde
wer-wolues þat wiln þe folk robben. / þe fend founded hem first
þe feiþ to destroie" (lines 459–60). Piers acknowledges that although
St. Dominic and St. Francis were good men who understood the
Gospel, their followers have fallen on evil ways. Moreover, they
have persecuted Wyclif "and oueral lollede him wiþ heretykes werkis"
(line 532), and they have viciously pursued another Wycliffite named
Walter Brute. The friars are like drones who eat up the first fruits.
Piers objects to the way that "lordes of the londe" honor such men
who would better "y-clense diches" (line 760) than be served with
silver. They should "deluen & diggen and dongen þe erþe" (line
785); their diet should be a "bolle-full of benen" rather than "per-
triches or plouers or pekokes yrosted" (line 764). In fact, they should
become vegetarians, as their founders were. Piers then teaches the
narrator the Creed and praises the Holy Presence in the sacrament,
which is "fullich his fleche and his blod" (line 823), a matter about
which friars foolishly dispute. The mystery cannot be explained — "it
is his blissed body, so bad he vs beleuen" (line 830).

Piers Plowman's Crede is an admirable mixture of Langland, Wyclif, and perhaps even Chaucer. Its plot grows directly out of Will's
search for St. Truth in *Piers Plowman* as he endeavors to find out
how to save his soul. Skeat ties the poem to the beginning of the
Vita section where Will, seeking Dowel, encounters two friars,
"Maistres of the menoures, men of grete witte" (B.VIII.9).[50] But
it is perhaps more instructive to think of *Piers Plowman's Crede* quite
literally as a sequel to *Piers Plowman*. At the end of Langland's poem
Conscience flees the House of Unity because it has become corrupted. Earlier, in an effort to stem the tide of Antichrist's hordes,
Conscience had invited "Frere Frauncys and Dominyk" into the
house (B.XX.251), only to be driven out himself by evil friars
who "wexeth out of noumbre," just as "helle is without noumbre"
(B.XX.267–68). In seeking Piers, Conscience hopes that the friars
might "hadde a fyndyng" (B.XX.381). In *Piers Plowman's Crede* it
is as if the narrator is the persona's personal Conscience who, like
Will's guide at the end of Langland's poem, seeks Piers, a man living in this world who can instruct him in true belief, but on the
way he encounters multitudes of friars in their "fyndyng," established throughout the world, as proud and as deceitful as ever. Certainly the narrator functions as a conscience figure as he knows
from the outset that he needs more than the ritualistic Ave and

Pater noster. In his encounters with the minorites he demonstrates further the abilities of good conscience as he clings to what the Gospels tell him and rejects the friars' foolishness. And by the end he does meet with Piers and learn the creed, even apart from the corrupted House of Unity.

The Wycliffite tradition may be seen in *Piers Plowman's Crede's* scathing attack on avarice, simony, and temporalities. The contrast between the opulent surroundings of luxurious churchmen and the poverty and need vividly depicted in hard-working Piers and his long-suffering family functions dramatically as a devastating criticism of the affluent friars and their abuse of all that money they collect. But the most damaging commentary against them comes from their own mouths as they divisively condemn each other and greedily scramble for more wealth to waste while the peasants they rob starve. The poet's charge that the poor are pillaged so that wealthy churchmen can get wealthier corresponds exactly to an apology attributed to Wyclif: "Swilk maner of men bigging [*building*] thus biggings semen to turn bred into stones; that is to sey, the bred of the pore, that is, almis beggid, into hepis of stonis, that is, into stonen howsis costly and superflew, and therfor they semen werrar [*worse*] than the fend, that askid stonis into bred."[51] The poet is knowledgeable of many features of the Wycliffite movement. Not only does he defend Wyclif and his follower Walter Brute from his persecutors, citing Gospel references as his primary authority; like Wyclif, he declares worthless the blessings of corrupt men. Perhaps his accusation that the friars are the guilty ones for denying the living presence in the Eucharist is deliberately perverse (that being the charge usually brought in more recent times against Wyclif). But it may well be that the Wyclif we know, with all his writings conveniently available in our libraries, is not the Wyclif the poet knew. The fact that the poet so strongly defends the Eucharist may simply be proof that there was considerable latitude of thought among Wycliffites in the 1390s and that many of them— men like Clanvowe and probably others of the so-called Lollard knights—were for the most part quite orthodox in matters of the sacraments. For the *Crede*-poet, at least, it is the friars who desecrate the sacraments, disputing the doctrine of the Holy Presence; the Wycliffites are the truly holy men.

The second Wycliffite poem of the 1390s I wish to consider, the *Plowman's Tale* (ca. 1395–1400?), attacks the established church

hierarchy more broadly than *Piers Plowman's Crede* does.[52] Although
the two poems may well be by the same author, as Skeat suggested,[53] the style and tone of the two are quite different. Struc-
turally the *Plowman's Tale* combines *chanson d'aventure* devices with
debate and some dialogue. Its prologue was apparently added by
sixteenth-century Reformation propagandists in order to attach the
work to Chaucer and thereby get it past the censors. Its dialect
and allusions are definitely of the 1390s, however. As a Wycliffite
work it is interesting in much the same way *Piers Plowman's Crede*
is. Like Wyclif, the poet fiercely attacks the papacy, insisting upon
Christ's poverty, which should be a priest's model. He is critical
of the great cost of church and priestly decoration: "Christ made
never no cathedrals, / Ne with him was no cardinall / Wyth a reed
hatte as usen mynstralls" (lines 313–15). He is, moreover, a paci-
fist, abhorring war, especially in the name of religion. Though he
supports the efficacy of the sacraments, he is chary, nonetheless.
The sacraments help heal the soul "*if* they ben used in good use"
(line 1194; italics mine). As in *Piers Plowman's Crede*, the poet implies that "if they ben used in [no] good use" they are worthless.
The opening of the poem bluntly divides society into those who
"have" and those who "have not"—a reminder that some of the
theoretical issues that John Ball considered are not yet dead. It is
noteworthy, however, that the attack on the moneyed establishment is carefully restricted to the second estate. Baronial holdings
are never challenged, which perhaps suggests a kinship with attitudes of the Lollard knights. Like *Piers Plowman's Crede*, the *Plowman's Tale* attacks official church policies of persecution. In these
days great churchmen—pope, bishops, cardinals, canons, parsons,
and vicars—who sell the sacraments as proudly as if they were
Lucifer, label as heretics "who-so speketh ayenst hir powere" (line
835). Were Christ to walk "on erthë here eft-soon, / These wolde
dampnë him to dye"; they would say "his sawes ben heresy" and
condemn his followers to be burned (lines 629ff.). Like the author
of *Piers Plowman's Crede*, the author of the *Plowman's Tale* knows his
Scripture well and interlaces his arguments with fundamental bib-
lical positions with which he would confound great churchmen.

The poet begins by observing a "sterne stryf" which is *once again*
stirring, as if to imply that in truth the strife has been simmering
a long time, at least, perhaps, since 1381. The one side (the haves)
consists of popes, cardinals, monks, friars, and such who allegedly

keep the keys to heaven and hell. The other side (the have-nots)
consists of "lollers and londlees" (line 73) — the poor who seek peace,
"semë caytifs sore a-cale" (line 71). The narrator, one of those truth-
seekers of the late fourteenth century, sets out through "many a
countrey" (line 77) hoping to determine which side is more false.
In a wood he encounters two birds, a Griffin and a Pelican, engaged in debate. The Griffin, "of a grim stature" (line 86), pleads
the pope's side; the Pelican, "withouten pryde / To these lollers
layde his lure" (line 88). The debate is quite one-sided, the Pelican
overwhelmingly carrying the day. His criticisms of the church are
commonplace, especially akin to Gower's. He attacks priests who
would be warriors ("They take on hem royáll powére, / And seye,
they have swerdes two, / Oon curse to helle, oon slee men here"
(lines 565–68). Perhaps he has in mind, as Gower did in the Prologue to the *Confessio Amantis*, the disastrous crusade against the
French led by the bishop of Norwich in 1382. Military priests are
traitors to Christ, he says, "as lowe as Lucifer such shal fall" (line
119). The two popes with their "crusades" are simply murderers:
"many a man is killed with knyf, / To wete which of hem have lordship shall" (lines 241–42). Like Gower, he cries out repeatedly
against simony. Christ bade Peter keep his sheep and forbade him
to smite with his sword. But popes now are false shepherds (lines
565ff.) who butcher the sheep and harm them "with greet dispyte"
(line 579). The pope culls them as a cook does, wastes their wool,
then justifies himself by falsely glossing "the gospell-book" (line 595).
When the Griffin defends papal "lordship" the Pelican utters "an
houge cry" (line 1109): there is but one Lord, one Christ; Christ
"bad his preestes no maystership have" (line 1122).

The conclusion to the poem is cleverly staged. The Pelican mod-
erates his caustic tone somewhat, explaining that he does not de-
spise the office of the papacy nor the sacraments, only the pope's
pride, his "richesse," his "wickednesse ... knowe so wyde" (line 1183).
A pope should live humbly, meekly, and in poverty, at which the
Griffin explodes:

> "Thou shalt be brent in balefull fyre;
> And all thy secte I shall distrye,
> Ye shal be hanged by the swyre!
> Ye shullen be hanged and to-drawe.
> Who giveth you leve for to preche

> Or speke agaynes goddes lawe
> And the people thus falsly teche?
> Thou shalt be cursed with boke and bell,
> And dissevered from holy churche,
> And clene ydampned into hell."
>
> (lines 1234–43)

The fearless Pelican calmly replies, "Your cursinge is of litell value" (line 1246). He will take his reward from God, not some Nero. God bade his servants to love, not hate. The Griffin defensively protects his pride by smiling: "The Griffon grinned as he were wood, / And loked lovely as an owle!" (line 1269). In a rage he departs to get an army of robbers and raviners to destroy the Pelican. While he is gone the Pelican converses with the Plowman (i.e., the narrator), explaining his iconography!

> For Christ him-selfe is lykned to me,
> That for his people dyed on rode;
> As fare I, right so fareth he,
> He fedeth his birdes with his blode.
>
> (lines 1293–96)

The horde of fiends return to an apocalyptic scene. The Pelican weeps at the thought of war, but suddenly a phoenix appears beside him, and the Griffin and his army are destroyed, driven under the earth where the narrator can still hear them yelling: "Alas! they had a feble grace!" The conclusion has a Chaucerian ring to it as the narrator, like the Nun's Priest in his fable, hides behind his fictitious bird: the words are the Pelican's; the poet is utterly orthodox![54]

The final Wycliffite work I wish to examine is *Jack Upland*, a prose treatise which survives in two manuscripts accompanied by other Wycliffite texts and in early printed editions, including Speght's second edition of Chaucer's *Works* (1602).[55] *Jack Upland* begins by lamenting the deceits and "fals signes" (line 3) of Antichrist which confuse so many. "But þe fellist folk þat euer Antecrist foond," the author says, "ben last brouзte into þe chirche, and in a wondir wise" (lines 69–70). They are the friars. Their infiltration into the church in the last days reminds one of *Piers Plowman*. Friars are obedient to no one: they neither "tilien ne sowen, weden ne repen, neþer whete, corn ne gras, ne good þat men schal help but oonli hem silf" (lines 73–75). The diverse sects claim "al maner power of God" and "sille heuene or helle to whom þat hem likiþ" (lines 75–77). The author, who calls himself Jack Upland, then poses sixty-four questions to the friars which expose, in his estimation, their corruption. The name "Jack Upland" seems designed to imply a rustic, perhaps one of Piers' good folk, a common man like those John Ball named in his epistles. The abuses Upland attacks are the same ones that other authors criticize: the fact that friars claim to be better confessors than secular priests, that they always need more money for their expensive buildings, that they prefer to dine graciously on fine food, that they boast the superiority of their "golden trentals" providing a good fee has been paid, that they insist that there are no friars in hell, that they prefer rich to poor company, that they insist on a mass penny before they will depart, that they pretentiously write the names of gift givers on tables as if the gift assured the giver's salvation, that they boast of their poverty while eagerly adding to their earthly treasures, that they invest so heavily in books, that they pride themselves on being the best beggars of the confraternity, and so on.[56] These kinds of abuses are the staple of confraternal satire.

According to P. L. Heyworth, "*Upland* must be among the earliest (and perhaps not quite the worst) of the stream of tracts that poured from semi-literate pens at the end of the fourteenth and throughout the fifteenth century."[57] The piece seems to have been well enough known; *Vae Octuplex*, which accompanies Wyclif's sermons in Douce 321, imitates it. About 1419 one "Friar Daw," who claims to have been "a manciple at Mertoun Halle," answers Upland's attack in *Friar Daw's Reply*.[58] A generation later (ca. 1450),[59] another work still is appended to *Upland*, this one being usually referred to as *Jack Upland's Rejoinder*. One marvels how a work as crude as *Jack Upland* could ever have gotten associated with Chaucer, aside from the fact that a little over half of his "questions" are raised in Chaucer's satiric treatment of friars. Indeed, how did the *Plowman's Tale* join his canon as well? That Reformation propagandists are responsible for the specific attributions is certainly true. But I think that more is involved, that the linking is not so utterly outlandish as it at first seems. We normally think of Chaucer and Langland as being in quite opposite traditions. But in fact, even at the beginning of the fifteenth century the separate literary traditions were being blended by penitential and political writers. The

Digby 102 manuscript is a case in point. We have already seen numerous instances in which the author of "Love God and Drede" draws upon Chaucer's moral balades. But although the poet writes primarily in 8-line stanzaic verse and draws thematic material from Chaucer, he also draws extensively from Langland for subject matter: witness such titles as "Mede and Muche Thank," "Wit and Will," and "Lerne say-welle, say littel, or say-noght." Like Langland and Langlandian poems such as *Richard the Redeless* and *Mum and the Sothesegger*, he uses particular political situations from which to generalize. His advice to rulers, attacks on simony, discussions of conscience and the importance of Truth reflect the taste of a literary circle which thrived on both Chaucer's French and the native alliterative traditions. It was a circle which had an abiding interest in political questions, reform, and penitential literature. The Digby 102 manuscript begins with the C-text of *Piers Plowman* (fols. 1–97), then includes the twenty-four political and penitential lyrics (fols. 98–127), which are followed by a metrical paraphrase of seven penitential Psalms by Richard Maydestone (fols. 128–35) and the *Debate of the Body and Soul* (fols. 136–39).

In brief, it is my contention that although the Reformation may be responsible for the actual attribution of *Jack Upland* and the *Plowman's Tale* to Chaucer, there is a long tradition going back to the late 1390s in which Chaucer and such alliterative poetry shared a common audience. We have seen how the Langland alliterative tradition made inroads in the court through the Advice-to-Princes genre, especially in works like *Richard the Redeless* and *Mum and the Sothesegger*. But the case can also be made for Chaucerian influence on poems like *Piers Plowman's Crede* and the *Plowman's Tale*. We have noted the Chaucerian ring to the conclusion of the *Plowman's Tale*. Earlier in the poem the Pelican echoes the *Pardoner's Tale* when he tells how evil papal representatives like pardoners "ransom" people by selling them worthless parchment without a thought of what might happen to their souls:

> A simple fornicacioun,
> Twenty shillings he shall pay:
> And then have an absolucioun,
> And al the yere usen it forth he may!
> Thus they letten hem go a-stray,
> They recke nat though the soul be brend.[60]
>
> (lines 669–74)

It is conceivable that *Piers Plowman's Crede* is also an example of Chaucerian influence on a Langlandian-Wycliffite poem, though both Chaucer and that poet are writing within a long-established tradition of anti-fraternal satire which Wycliffite teachings helped to rejuvenate. It is remarkable how many satiric points the two authors share. In both, friars claim their prayers more potent than those of others because of the antiquity of their order, prayers so potent that they may be substituted for an individual's performing of penitential acts on his own; gifts to the brotherhood make the giver a brother and thus guarantee his salvation. Both poets satirize confraternal pomp, lechery, and gluttony, singling out the friars' preference for comfortable houses and gourmet food. Both have their friars pervert St. Paul's comments on the "first fruits" as they boast about their privileges. Both ridicule inner fraternal rivalry and backbiting and the eagerness with which friars solicit money for their buildings. More specifically, both pun on the term "fundament," dress their fat friars in "double worsted," comment on the bench where friars sit, and use Phil. 3:18 to describe the glutton's practice of making a god of his belly. And, like Chaucer's wicked ecclesiasts, the friars in *Piers Plowman's Crede* rob the poor, regardless of how needy they are. None of these parallels is sufficiently exact to prove conclusively that the author of *Piers Plowman's Crede* drew on Chaucer, but one is struck by the frequency with which Chaucer comes to mind in reading any of the three anti-clerical pieces which we have been considering.

The linking of Chaucer with the Wycliffite poems is less outrageous than it at first seems when we recall that Chaucer probably wrote the Marriage group, which includes the *Friar's* and the *Summoner's Tales*, as well as the lively exchange between the Wife of Bath and the Pardoner, during the years 1393–1395, that is, at about the same time or slightly before these Wycliffite works were written. In the later 1390s Chaucer's marriage group may not have been viewed as a marriage group at all (the term is Kittredge's),[61] but rather as a churchmen group. Or, if it is a marriage group, it is about marriage in the same way that the Lady Meed sections of *Piers Plowman* are about marriage. Though the Wife of Bath is the dominant figure in this group she is surrounded by ecclesiasts— the Pardoner, Friar, Summoner, and Clerk. She is herself a kind of Meed figure with her love of goods, her scarlet clothes and ten pounds of kerchiefs, a figure who sets the Friar, Summoner, and Pardoner in competition for her attention, or, at least, for atten-

tion. Rather than debate with Conscience about marriage, as Lady
Meed does in *Piers*, Dame Alice debates with St. Paul,[62] twisting
his conscientious ethics on chastity to her own peculiar warp. In
her prologue she tells how she would marry an Oxford clerk and
how he, tempted by her dream of blood and gold, would marry
her. The Clerk of Oxford on the pilgrimage has a more scrupu-
lous conscience than Alisoun's Jankyn and uses his tale of Griselde,
who in Chaucer's day would surely have been glossed as a figure
of Holy Church, as a rhetorically skillful means of rejecting the
Wife's worldly claims. The satire on the Friar and Summoner,
representing two competing divisions of the fiendishly corrupted
Christian establishment, are placed at the center of the group. Combined with the *Pardoner's Tale*, they remain the most brilliant satires on ecclesiastical corruption to come from the period and are
quite enough in themselves to win Chaucer the reputation of reformer which he carried with him into the Renaissance.

Epilogue

Though it is often said that little came of the Peasant's Revolt,
it seems to me that a great deal originated there, much of which
took shape as a subject, at least, if not a completed sentence, in
the decades immediately following 1381. Moreover, that subject
affected the actions of men even in distant generations to come.
The subject of church reform found its verb in the sixteenth century where links with fourteenth-century thought were not only explicit but extensive. Propagandists published their polemics in the
name of Chaucer and Langland;[63] Foxe called Chaucer "a right
Wiclifian," an idea that so caught on that, in view of Chaucer's
many brilliant attacks on ecclesiastical corruption (including the
Plowman's Tale and *Jack Upland* which become associated with him),
by the seventeenth century Vaughan could assert that Chaucer
was Wyclif's master.[64] Though the Renaissance does Chaucer a
disfavor by imposing upon him works as crude as *Jack Upland*,
there is a kind of justice in the fact that the principal half-dozen
satires on church abuses from the end of the fourteenth century,
including the C-fragment of "Chaucer's" *Romaunt of the Rose* (lines
5811–7696), are brought together again 150 years later under the
name of the greatest author among them.[65] Though Foxe's label-
ling of that author as a "right Wiclifian" is probably inaccurate,

it is nonetheless true that Chaucer flourished among Wycliffians
and that they bore him good company and good will.

The linking of the Peasant's Revolt and revolution does not end
with the Reformation. The political reforms at the end of the eight-
eenth century likewise look back to the Peasant's Revolt to some
extent, not for the support of monarchy in a Wycliffite vein, however, but for inspirational martyrs of democracy. Robbins has commented on Tom Payne's use of Wat Tyler and John Ball in support of the American cause[66] and on the "ghost of Langland" which
"stands behind Lilburne, and the ghost of Wyclif behind Winstan-
ley. One might fantasize that the Lollard Payne was reincarnated
four hundred years later with the same surname."[67] Robbins concludes his essay on the spirit of reform with the words of William
Grindecobbe, a man of great conscience who was executed after
the 1381 revolt at St. Albans: "Fellow citizens, you whom a new-
born freedom has released from longstanding oppression, stand firm
while you can. Have no fear of my execution. And if I must die,
I shall count myself happy to end my life by such a martyrdom."[68]

But perhaps the most insidious revolution to germinate in England in the latter days of the fourteenth century is what Professor
Robertson, who, I am certain, would not agree with my present
premise, has termed Romanticism, though he would perhaps agree
that Romanticism, more than anything else, marks the shift from
medieval to modern consciousness. But if my interpretation of the
vernacular penitential movement, the new vernacular meanings
of conscience, and the growth of individualism is accurate, the first
slopes of that watershed are to be found in the period surrounding
and immediately following 1381. As with the Reformation polem-
icists, the English apologists for Romanticism — Godwin, Leigh
Hunt, William Hazlitt, Charles Cowden Clarke, Robert Southey,
and so on — turn Chaucer into a champion of human rights, linking him once again with Wyclif.[69] Leigh Hunt praises him as one
who was "unequivocally on the side of freedom, and helped pro-
cure us our present enjoyments."[70] Like the Reformation writers,
the Romantic authors perceive a Chaucer who wrote the *Testament
of Love* from prison and the *Plowman's Tale* in the fervent spirit of
reform. We now know that the *Testament of Love* was by Chaucer's
friend Thomas Usk, a victim of the "Merciless Parliament," and
the *Plowman's Tale* by a Langlandian-Wycliffite reformer. Whatever truth there is in the Romantic assessments, it must be said

to come from a blended tradition of Wyclif, Langland and Chaucer, not from any one poet. But it bears the unique marks of the social conscience of late fourteenth-century literary men, nonetheless, a conscience which had much in common with the less verbal but more daring convictions of John Ball.

Notes

1. "John Ball's Letters: 1381," in Rossell Hope Robbins, ed., *Historical Poems of the Fourteenth and Fifteenth Centuries* (New York, 1959), pp. 54–55. The second letter appears first in the St. Albans Chronicle (Royal MS. 13.E.ix) and also in Thomas Walsingham's *Historia Anglicana* 2:34 and the *Chronicon Angliae*. Both are included in John Stow's *Annales* (1580; 1615). On the commonplace matter of these poems see Rossell Hope Robbins, "Middle English Poems of Protest," *Anglia* 78 (1960): 193–203. Robbins observes, "Previously many had lamented these conditions; Ball was the first to want to do something about them" (p. 201).

2. All *Piers Plowman* quotations are taken either from the B- or C-texts edited by W. W. Skeat, *The Vision of William Concerning Piers the Plowman in Three Parallel Texts*, 2 vols. (Oxford, 1924), and are cited in context by text and line.

3. Vincent DiMarco, *Piers Plowman: A Reference Guide* (Boston, 1982), p. 1, cites the will of Walter de Bruge, 1395, as the first mention of *Piers Plowman*. Ball's letter precedes de Bruge's will by ca. fourteen years.

4. Robbins, *Historical Poems*, p. 61.

5. *Confessio Amantis*, Prologus, 851. Cf. Prol. 28–30, 125–28, 331–37, and 641–1052 *passim*, but especially 641–50, 851–55, 893–95, 967–73, 983–1001, 1008–16, 1022–25, 1029–30. All references to the *Confessio Amantis* are taken from G. C. Macaulay, ed., *The English Works of John Gower*, 2 vols. (London, 1900).

6. All references to Chaucer's works are taken from F. N. Robinson, ed., *The Works of Geoffrey Chaucer*, 2nd ed. (Cambridge, Mass., 1957), and will be cited by work and line number in the context of my argument.

7. Initially Gower combines the passage from John 8:32 with the passage Chaucer uses in his poem "Truth: Balade of Good Counsel": "Senec conseileth in this wise ... 'Bot if thi good suffise / Unto the liking of thi wille, / Withdrawh thi lust and hold the stille, / And be to thi good sufficant.' / For that thing is appourtenant / To trouthe and causeth to be fre / After the reule of charite, / Which ferst beginneth of himselve" *CA* V.7735–43. (Gower's attribution to Seneca is inaccurate; the saying rather derives from Caecilius Balbus, *De Nugis Philosophorum* XI.) Gower goes on to cite Truth as the primary point of policy in which a king should be instructed *CA* VII.1711–1984.

8. In his advice to the boy-king Richard, Gower makes the same point emphatically: "It is better for you, O king, to govern yourself according to the law than to subjugate all ... to yourself.... You who conquer others, strive to conquer yourself.... You who subdue others, work to subdue yourself. If you wish to be a king, rule yourself, and you will be one" (*Vox Clamantis*, Bk. VI, chap. 8). The translation is from *The Major Latin Works of John Gower*, trans. Eric W. Stockton (Seattle, 1962), p. 234.

9. Something of the idealism of the peasant leaders may be seen in the destruction of Gaunt's Savoy Palace, where the rebels were forbidden to loot. According to Knighton, *Chronicon Henrici Knighton*, Rolls Series, vol. 92 (London, 1895), 2:135, one man who tried to steal a piece of silver was thrown into the fire to be burned with his loot, as if to make the point that the zealots were upholders of truth and justice, not thieves. Cf. Ball's chastising of "hobbe þe robbere" in his second epistle.

10. The phrase comes from Caxton and other early chroniclers to designate the turmoil of the Peasants' Revolt. Cf., Caxton, *The Cronicles of Englond* (1480) 239:264, and Robert Fabyan, *The Newe Cronycles of Englande and of Fraunce* (1516) 7:531, as cited by the *OED*. Charles Oman, *The Great Revolt of 1381* (Oxford, 1906), p. 77, notes the phrase in Gregory's *Chronicle* as well.

11. Rossell Hope Robbins, "Dissent in Middle English Literature," *Medievalia et Humanistica* 9 (1979): 27.

12. Ibid., p. 28.

13. Ibid., pp. 34-35.

14. John Wyclif, *Select English Works of John Wyclif*, ed. Thomas Arnold (Oxford, 1871), 3:407. The sentiment is distinctly Wyclif's, though the phrase may be from one of his followers. It comes from *De Blasphemia Contra Fratres*, Bodl. 647, which Bale attributes to Wyclif. Arnold prints the work under "Controversial Tracts," though he is disposed to think it Wyclif's.

15. Robbins, "Dissent in Middle English," p. 35.

16. K. B. McFarlane, *Lancastrian Kings and Lollard Knights* (Oxford, 1972), pp. 140-44.

17. Marjorie Anderson, "Blanche, Duchess of Lancaster," *MP* 45 (1948): 157-59.

18. George B. Pace, "Speght's Chaucer and [Cambridge University Library] MS Gg.4.27," *SB* 21 (1968): 225-35.

19. Contemporary chroniclers praise Anne for her education and piety (cf. *Hist. Ang.* 2:46; Knighton 2:150; Higden 9:12). She was patron of the Eye priory and joint founder, with Richard, of the Coventry charterhouse (May McKisack, *The Fourteenth Century: 1307-1399* [Oxford, 1959], pp. 294n, 295). Gardiner Stillwell, "The Political Meaning of Chaucer's Tale of Melibee," *Speculum* 19 (1944): 433-44, suggests that her influence on Richard's peace policies may be figured in Dame Prudence. McKisack argues that Anne cannot have been sympathetic with Lollard causes because of Richard's antipathy toward them (*Fourteenth Century*, p. 427), but we must keep in mind that the king's antipathy was mainly expressed after the presenting of the Twelve Conclusions to Parliament and the posting of them on the door of St. Paul while he was away in 1395 (after Anne's death), fighting in Ireland. His anger against his privy counsellors reflects mainly his frustration in Ireland and

---

his resentment at having been recalled to look after his own ministers. By this time in his life, he was becoming increasingly autocratic and arbitrary. Although nothing indicates that he was himself in any way unorthodox, the fact remains that several Lollard knights were close to him in the early 1390s and were influential in advising peace policies with France. As he fought his war with the Irish their advocacy of peace was less welcome counsel.

20. McFarlane, *Lancastrian Kings*, pp. 135–226, explores the relationship between Lollard knights and court most fully. See also W. T. Waugh, "The Lollard Knights," *Scottish Historical Review* 11 (1913–1914): 55–92, and G. M. Trevelyan, *England in the Age of Wycliffe* (London, 1899), pp. 327–31.

21. The phrase is the introductory formula to several versions of the popular "Quia amore langueo" poems. (Cf. Cambridge University Library MS Hh.4.12 and Lambeth MS 853; printed in F. J. Furnivall, ed., *Political, Religious, and Love Poems*, EETS, o.s. vol. 15 [London, 1866]; also in Robert D. Stevick, *One Hundred Middle English Lyrics* [Indianapolis, 1964], pp. 88–93.) The phrase epitomizes admirably the trope of anxiety to which medieval dream and philosophical poetry so often addresses itself.

22. Robbins, "Dissent in Middle English Literature," p. 40; McFarlane, *Lancastrian Kings*, p. 209. For fourteenth-century responses see the defense of English translation attributed to John Purvey in the Middle English translation of Wyclif's *De Officio Pastorali*: "Heere the freris with their fautours seyn that it is heresye to write thus Goddis lawe in English and make it knowun to lewid men.... It semyth first that the wit of Goddis lawe shulde be taught in that tunge that is more knowun, for this wit is Goddis word.... As lordis of Englond han the Bible in Freynsch, so it were not ayenus resoun that they hadden the same sentense in Engliysch.... Why may not al be turnyd to Engliysch trewely ... specialy sithen alle Cristen men, lerid and lewid, that shulen be savyd moten algatis sue Crist and knowe his lore and his lif. But the comyns of Engliyschmen knowen it best in ther modir tunge, and thus it were al oon to lette siche knowing of the Gospel and to lette Engliysch men to sue Crist and come to hevene" (*The English Works of Wyclif*, ed. F. D. Matthew, EETS, o.s. vol. 74 [London, 1880], p. 429).

23. The appearance of "Boke that highte beuper" occurs at the climax of the *Vita* section of *Piers Plowman*, as the old law is fulfilled through the crucifixion and resurrection, as if to assert that Scripture is what we now have for guidance. On the role of vernacular penitential manuals in fourteenth-century spiritual history and their challenge to authority see Francis Hildahl, "Authority, Power, and Influence: Dimensions of Meaning in *The Castle of Perseverance*" (Ph.D. diss., University of Rochester, 1985).

24. Cf. *ParsT* 115–16, 314 on grace; 115–20, 382–83 on burning love of God; 415–30 on superfluity of dress (cf. Lollard conclusion twelve); 575–77 against birth control and child abandonment (cf. Lollard conclusion eleven); 1013–15 on the necessary fidelity of the priest (cf. Harry Bailly's fear of damnation should he submit to the false Pardoner — "Nay, nay ... thanne have I Cristes curs" VI [C] 946). See H. S. Cronin, "The Twelve Conclusions of the Lollards," *English Historical Review* 22 (1907): 292–304, for Roger Dymok's presentation of the Conclusions both in English and Latin, excerpted from his *Against the XII Heresies of the Lollards*, which he presented to Richard II upon

his return from Ireland, ca. 1396-1397. The English version seems to be the words of the Lollards themselves, the Latin Dymok's translation. A Latin version may also be found in the *Fasciculi Zizaniorum,* Rolls Series, vol. 5 (London, 1858), pp. 360-69.

25. *Pierce the Ploughmans Crede,* ed. Walter W. Skeat (London, 1867), p. 20, where the poet tells how friars "overal lolled him [Wyclif] wiþ heretykes werkes" when he "warned hem wiþ trewþe" (lines 528-32).

26. McFarlane, *Lancastrian Kings,* pp. 207-20.

27. *OED* (1933), 2:845.

28. Alexander Cruden, *A Complete Concordance to the Holy Scriptures of the Old and New Testament* (New York, 1871), p. 93.

29. See Russell A. Peck, "St. Paul and the *Canterbury Tales,*" *Revue l'Université d'Ottawa* 53 (1983): 414.

30. Iohannis Wyclif, *Tractatus de Officio Regis,* ed. Alfred W. Pollard and Charles Sayle (London, 1887), pp. 57-59, 237.

31. Willi Erzgräber, *William Langlands Piers Plowman* (*eine interpretation des C-textes*). Frankfurter Arbeiten aus dem Gebiete der Anglistik und der Amerika-Studien, heft 3, (Heidelberg, 1957), pp. 106-8.

32. *Twenty-Six Political and other Poems (Including 'Petty Job') from the Oxford MSS. Digby 102 and Douce 322,* ed. Dr. J. Kail (London, 1904), pp. x-xi.

33. As cited by Anna Baldwin, *The Theme of Government in Piers Plowman* (Cambridge, 1981), p. 10; *De Officio Regis,* p. 97 (see also pp. 118-45).

34. Margaret E. Aston, "Lollardy and Sedition 1381-1431," *Past and Present* 17 (1960): 1-44. See especially the Chronicles of Knighton, Walsingham, and the Dominican Roger Dymoke, who complained in 1395 that by such Wycliffite principles as those undermining the church "no one thence forward in this kingdom would possess his lordships in safety, since anybody would be able to rise against another when he wished" (Aston, n. 38).

35. The anticlerical document by two friars is reprinted by Vivian H. Galbraith, "Articles Laid Before the Parliament of 1371," *English Historical Review* 34 (1919): 579-82.

36. McKisack, *The Fourteenth Century,* p. 290.

37. Though Richard lost the struggle for absolute sovereignty, the Wycliffite principles from which he worked were adopted by Henry, with slightly better success. Richard acted too arbitrarily too often without paying sufficient heed to baronial counsel. Repeatedly, the charges against him, whether in Parliament, the chronicles, or in political poetry at the end of the century like Gower's *Tripartite Chronicle* and *Richard the Redeless,* were that he was too arrogant, that he squandered the wealth of the state on favorites in his livery, that he elevated men regardless of station into positions of high counsel—lewed men like Burley, Green, Bushy, and Bagot who flattered him with notions of autonomy—rather than following wiser and older men of good breeding, who would have better protected hereditary rights and baronial independence.

38. McFarlane, *Lancastrian Kings,* pp. 36-42.

39. Baldwin, *Theme of Government,* especially pp. 15-23 on Reason, Conscience, absolutism, and problems of authority; and pp. 39-54 on the triumph of authority. Meed, Baldwin observes on p. 1, "represents a serious late me-

dieval problem.... Langland [following Wyclif's absolutist principles] indicates
how it might be solved when the '*Visio* king' asserts his prerogative right to
replace the corrupted Common Law by Natural Law principles voiced by
Reason and Conscience. (This was precisely the solution which Richard's
government also attempted — though with less success.)"

40. Ibid., p. 23.

41. Ibid.

42. Ibid., p. 38.

43. Ibid.

44. Skeat, *The Vision of William Concerning Piers the Plowman*, 1:619.

45. Cf. Ockham, *Reportatio*, 3. q. 11.x: *Recta autem ratio est prudentia in actu
vel in habitu.*

46. See Russell A. Peck, *Kingship and Common Profit in Gower's Confessio Amantis* (Carbondale, 1978), p. 197 n. 1, and Fritz Schulz, "Bracton on Kingship,"
English Historical Review 60 (1945): 153, 156–69.

47. The date is Skeat's, *Pierce the Ploughmans Crede (About 1394 A. D.).* "The
poem was certainly written after the latter part of 1393, and before 1401....
Internal evidence alone suggests some year in the series 1394–1399 as the year
of composition" (p. xi).

48. *Political Poems* (1832), as cited by Skeat, p. xiii. Wright thought the author to have been a Franciscan novice who left the confraternity to become
a Wycliffite. Skeat argues that the author is the same person who wrote the
Plowman's Tale, which he dates in the later 1390s, ca. 1395 (p. xvi). See n.
53 below.

49. All quotations from *PPC* are taken from Skeat's edition (1867; reprint,
New York, 1969).

50. Ibid., p. 33.

51. Ibid., p. 37.

52. All quotations from the *Plowman's Tale* are taken from W. W. Skeat's
edition in *Chaucerian and Other Pieces*, vol. 7 of *The Complete Works of Geoffrey
Chaucer* (Oxford, 1897), pp. 147–90.

53. Skeat, *PPC*, p. xvi. Skeat's argument favoring common authorship is
plausible. He notes the common dialect, vocabulary, numerous parallels in
phrasing, and explicit allusions in *PlT* to *PPC*. The fact that *PlT* is so thoroughly Wycliffite and yet deals so sparsely with friars lends credence to the
idea that they are omitted because the poet has so thoroughly belabored friars
in *PPC*. If Skeat is right, the poet we are dealing with is an unusually versatile
craftsman, having mastered Langland's alliterative line in *PPC* and also a
courtly 8-line stanza (ababbcbc) in *PlT*. In the latter poem he uses a refrain
line in each of the first sections, which means that the same c-rhyme runs
throughout each section (i.e., a span of 700 lines).

54. Cf., *NPT* VII (B2) 3265: "Thise been the cokkes wordes, and nat myne."

55. Skeat includes *JU* in *Chaucerian and Other Pieces* (*Works*, 7:191–203); he
uses the 1536 black letter edition, along with Speght 1598 as his copy texts.
The edition I follow here is that of P. L. Heyworth, *Jack Upland, Friar Daw's
Reply, and Upland's Rejoinder* (London, 1968). Two manuscripts survive (BM
MS Harley 6641 and Cambridge University Library MS Ff.vi.2) which Skeat
did not know and which differ considerably from the 1536 black letter edi-

tion. Heyworth provides a critical text of the version in the manuscripts, using 1536 and the text underlying *Friar Daw's Reply* as guides to conjecture in
places where the MSS seem corrupt. Anne Hudson, " 'No newe thyng': The
Printing of Medieval Texts in the Early Reformation Period," in *Middle English Studies Presented to Norman Davis in Honour of his Seventieth Birthday*, ed. Doug-
las Gray and E. G. Stanley (Oxford, 1983), pp. 153–74, notes an early Latin
translation of the work also, of which Heyworth makes no mention.

56. I deliberately cite those offenses in the list which also appear in Chaucer's lampoon in the *Friar's Tale* and the *Summoner's Tale*, works which were
probably composed ca. 1393–94 (i.e., prior to *JU*). Another work hostile to
friars that may have been done about this time is the C-fragment of the *Romaunt* (attributed to Chaucer), which translates into Chaucer's dialect Jean
de Meun's satire against the confraternities.

57. Heyworth, *Jack Upland* p. 18. Heyworth qualifies his clever label "semi-
literate" as perhaps too pejorative; "workaday academic" would probably be
more apt.

58. Ibid., line 725. Although the claim of "manciple at Mertoun Halle" is
probably simply a literary device to account for the quantity of Latin used
in Friar Daw's refutation, the association with Merton is curious, in view of
Chaucer's apparent connections there through Strode and others. (Cf. J. A.
W. Bennett's chapter "The Men of Merton" in *Chaucer at Oxford and at Cambridge* [Toronto, 1974], pp. 58–87, which demonstrates how frequently Chaucer's intellectual trails lead to Merton.) The author of *FDR* is far from "semi-
literate"; rather he is a skillful rhetorician and learned man who knows in-
timately the history of confraternal pamphleteering and the heresies of "þat
wickide worme – Wiclyf be his name" (line 71). Heyworth suggests that he
may be a Dominican.

59. The date is Heyworth's.

60. Cf. Chaucer's Pardoner's not caring whether his victims' "soules goon
a-blakeberyed" (VI [C] 406) and the Summoner's finding "simple fornicacioun"
the most lucrative of punishable sins (III [D] 1310).

61. George Kittredge, *Chaucer and his Poetry* (Cambridge, Mass., 1915), pp.
185–211.

62. See my "St. Paul and the *Canterbury Tales*," pp. 420–23.

63. On censorship and Reformation attitudes toward Chaucer see Andrew
Wawn's three essays, "The Genesis of the *Plowman's Tale*," *YES* 2 (1972): 21–40;
"Chaucer, Wyclif, and the Court of Apollo," *ELN* 10 (1972): 15–20; and
"Chaucer, *The Plowman's Tale* and Reformation Propaganda: The Testimonies
of Thomas Godfray and *I Playne Piers*," *BJRL* 56 (1973–1974): 174–92. See
also Russell A. Fraser's discussion of Renaissance censorship in his introduc-
tion to his edition of *The Court of Venus* (Durham, 1955), and Margaret Aston,
"Lollardy and the Reformation: Survival or Revival," *History* 49 (1964): 149–70.

64. Wawn, "Chaucer, Wyclif, and the Court of Apollo," p. 17.

65. W. W. Skeat, *The Chaucer Canon* (Oxford, 1900), dates the translation
of the C-fragment of the *Romaunt* in the early 1390s; he emphasizes the trans-
lator's attraction to religious satire and identifies him as "one who sympathized,
probably, with the author of *The Plowman's Tale*" (p. 93).

66. Robbins, "Dissent in Middle English Literature," pp. 25–26.

67. Ibid., p. 42.

68. Ibid.

69. Francis W. Bonner, "Chaucer's Reputation During the Romantic Period," *Furman Studies* 34 (1951): 1–21.

70. Leigh Hunt, "Essay on the Poetical Character," *The Round Table* 1 (1817): 186, as cited by Bonner, p. 11.

The papers included in **Social Unrest in the Late Middle Ages** were the major presentations given at the Fifteenth Annual CEMERS Conference, sponsored by the Center for Medieval and Early Renaissance Studies at the University Center at Binghamton on October 16–17, 1981.

The papers included in this volume reflect the range of topic and approach that characterized the conference as a whole. John Block Friedman finds that the artists often used traditional images of death to depict this catastrophe by indirection. Through a careful study of the records of peasant hostility to oppression, Barbara Hanawalt demonstrates that the Revolt of 1381 was only the most dramatic manifestation of a wider pattern of social change. Russell A. Peck studies the Wycliffite writings that appeared in England following the Peasants' Revolt (1381) and their impact on the sensibility of the major poets of the era—Glover, Langland and Chaucer. J. Ambrose Raftis explores new methods of investigation derived from the social sciences, which may be brought to bear on interpretation of events. D. W. Robertson discusses the sense of moral failure which was widespread in late 14th-century England, and which is exemplified in Chaucer's *Prologue to the Canterbury Tales*.

Francis X. Newman is Associate Professor of English and Chairman of the Cinema department at the University Center at Binghamton, N.Y. He is the editor of *The Meaning of Courtly Love*.

mrts

medieval & renaissance texts & studies
is the publishing program of the
Center for Medieval & Early Renaissance Studies
at the University Center at Binghamton.

mrts emphasizes books that are needed —
texts, translations, and major research tools.

mrts aims to publish the highest quality scholarship
in attractive and durable format at modest cost.

DATE DUE